DEDICATION

To every husband and wife that remains true to their commitment to each other, their children, and God Almighty who ultimately will judge all according to His Word. I pray that God continues to bless and protect your marriage for you are the foundation of societies that this book has been written for.

FORWARD

First off I want to thank and congratulate you for purchasing the book "Overcoming 50 Shades of Grey And All The Colors Of The LGBT Rainbow." Your continued support for the American Christian Defense Alliance, Inc. books are greatly appreciated as well as your prayers for our Ministry.

This book is in response to the continual onslaught of the Militant LGBT community and their war on the Biblical order of things. It is clear to see in our nation and throughout the world that the rise of the Militant LBGT community is moving at an ever increasing pace, being endorsed by the mass media, as well as corrupt politicians and judges.

Overcoming 50 Shades of Grey and All the Colors of the LGBT Rainbow

By: Patrick Baldwin

Special Request

Thank you for purchasing our book and supporting our Ministry. We have a Special Request for those that have purchased this book on the Kindle platform. We wanted to make you aware that Amazon's Kindle platform pays per pages "read". Our Special Request is that if you appreciate our Ministry's efforts to put out books such as this or if you would simply like to support our Ministry's work to please scroll to the back of the book, even if you don't "read" the book right away. This is how we will get paid through the paid per pages criteria.

We all lead such busy lives nowadays and can get side tracked so easily please take a moment to support us now by allowing us to be paid by scrolling to the end of the book – Then go back and read it at your leisure.

We deeply appreciate Your support and know that God will Bless You as You have Blessed this Ministry.

This book is an attempt to give the born again Christian believer the tools they need to overcome the lust of the flesh as well as tactics that the Militant LGBT community is imposing specifically in the United States of America. It is no secret that towards the end of any civilization or empire, demise lewdness, lust, and the quest for even more power prevail. It is also no secret that no nation has lasted forever, not even Rome in all its splendor is still around. So for the Christian seeking to walk in the fruits of the Spirit it is critical to learn how to be in the world, but not of the world.

In June of 2015 I personally went down to Washington DC when the call went out for Christians to rally for Solemn Assembly in front of the Supreme Court on the Hagman and Hagman radio show. Walking around the Supreme Court seven times with a backpack full gear in the blistering heat was not an ideal situation – yet this is what I did while praising and worshiping God listening to Carmen songs. My wife and young daughter also did about three laps around the Supreme Court too.

I felt it imperative to do what I could when I could to take a stand, not physically as it were but in the spirit. For what does the Scripture say – "We wrestle not against flesh and blood. . . ." There is actually a video of our trip to DC on our You Tube Page – Check it out when you can. If you attended that Assembly and are wondering if you meet me down there, I was the one who brought the Appeal To Heaven flag.

Some might argue or suggest why should we care what two consenting adults are doing in the bedroom. And to that I would say you're absolutely correct. I do not care what consenting adults do in their own bedrooms. But when their behavior and their actions affect my family and me, specifically my child I have a real issue with it. What the Militant LGBT Community is attempting to do is sexualize kids at younger ages regardless of parental control, opinion or belief. Now one has to ask themselves, why?

Is it merely a self-involved movement driven by the "love", passion, and desire to be with whomever they wish with no political or social goals – of course not, there is a bigger picture here. I will leave it up to you to conclude what that bigger picture is.

Nowadays you can't even turn on the television, radio, or go to a mall without seeing or hearing Militant LGBT propaganda. As a Christian father I have a duty and responsibility to train up my child in the way that they should go, yet at every turn the Militant LGBT community attempts to circumvent my God-given authority by pumping my child's head full of their propaganda – enough is enough. As a parent regardless of your belief system you should not have to be subjected or deal with attacks on your child's emotional, psychological, or Spiritual well being such as this on a continual basis.

As parents when someone takes away your rights, your God-given rights to teach and train your child in the way that you wish for them to be raised that should raise red flags for every decent parent out there. That is Your Child, not the states, not the schools, not the social workers – that is Your Child and You have a God-given responsibility and duty to provide and protect your child in every in any way possible. Now by all means I'm not suggesting that you live in such a manner to completely isolate your child, however, proactive approaches to minimizing the effects of the Militant LGBT community can be accomplished with very little effort. One such proactive approach is homeschooling your child - this is one of the fundamental ways to provide a solid education for your child as well as protect them from being indoctrinated in local government schools with political agendas. The American Christian Defense Alliance, Inc. does have a homeschool umbrella for those interested in homeschooling in Maryland just check out our website. We also highly recommend the Ron Paul Curriculum online.

This book will serve as a guide to help explain to you the notions behind 50 shades of Grey and all the Colors of Militant LGBT rainbow movement and how they are negatively affecting the Christian Community as well as our societies at large so we can overcome them. For those that don't know 50 shades of Grey, is a novel that promotes a sexual lifestyle and various acts towards your partner; particularly to a female partner and is creating a lot of confusion, especially among our youth as to what is acceptable.

Also explained in this book are issues as to the rise of the Militant "colors" of the LGBT rainbow, which refers to the movement that supports the blasphemous same sex relationships including transsexual and bisexual variations. This book has been written for the Christian Community to fight back against these demonic spirits that are infecting the land we occupy.

Back in day these acts were rare, abominations, and quite unheard of in most parts of the word – Yet here we are Today, just look around to see how far we have fallen. This is Our Country and It's Time to Take it Back. However, we must all realize at its core this is a Spiritual War and we can only be victorious if we walk in the Spirit of God. Realistically, if we don't do something fast God's judgment will fall upon as a nation – We can see this if we look back in history and note what happen when a nation turned from God.

Nowadays, the ideas that these movements promote are subjects of contention with so many different people having different opinions on them. The main aim of this book as I mentioned is to help as many Christians as possible overcome the influence and manipulation promoted by these groups and the workers of the devil who continue to try to lead the inhabitants of this world towards hell - yet are nothing more then pawns in the grand chess game of life. However, the change must start within our own hearts first.

As a Christian, it is important to note that if you are among those that would label themselves as 'liberal' Christians and support these groups to receive the approval of the world, the blessing of the evil one if you would, then you should know by now that you have been seriously mislead and deceived. You need to understand that our God is a jealous God. He is particularly jealous over you with godly jealousy, you cannot label yourself a Christian and at the same time seek the approval of those of the world. Those who feel the need to be loved by the world will do anything just to be accepted by the people of the world – and the Love of the Father is not in them.

We all need to stand up both individual and together and fight this tsunami of decadence before we are all washed away - it is no longer just some 'problem' we have to deal with.

We need to have a faith and assert our beliefs without fear of how our decisions to fight against these groups are viewed; this book will act as a guide to open your eyes to the real situation that is currently taking place in our society and suggest effective means that we as Christians can use in order to overcome this adversity. Jesus handed over the authority that he had to His Believers when He firmly declared, "Behold, I give unto you power to tread on serpents and scorpions, and over all the power of the enemy: and nothing shall by any means hurt you" (Luke 10:19).

In this book you will find hope and solutions to give the Christian believer, the Christian Parent, and the Christian Solider for Christ a solid framework to do battle and overcome 50 shades of gray and all the colors of the Militant LGB T rainbow. The Spirit of the Lord give you revelation and guidance as you read this book and search for answers – God bless you all.

TABLE OF CONTENTS

CHAPTER 1: LAWLESSNESS IN AMERICA

SPIRITUAL ROOTS OF THE MILITANT LGBT MOVEMENT

Lawlessness in America centers around the mystery of the lawless one. Lawlessness in the United States of America did not begin with the Supreme Court's opinion to condone same-sex unions it began long ago in ancient times. The mystery of the coming of the lawless one is in fact the mystery of the coming of antichrist and all of his workers. However, we know in the last days doctrines of demons will be prevalent, false teachers will arise proclaiming good to be evil and evil good, and that men will always love darkness rather than light because their deeds are evil so we must be vigilant and follow the commandment to watch and pray.

The spiritual roots of the spirits that cause men and women to seek pleasure within the same biological sex has throughout history plague societies yet there has always been a remnant, a group of God-fearing men and women to stand fast against them in prayer. It is once again time for this remnant of God to rise up and to proclaim boldly the word of God while sharing the love, compassion, and kindness that indicate we are in fact followers of Jesus Christ. As Christians is very important to operate out of a spirit of love, we must guard against our love growing cold. Now understand this our love can grow cold against the world as well as one another. Therefore, it's ever important to seek the face of God on a daily basis, to be in prayer, to read his word and then to exercise our faith with boldness and conviction but most importantly love. 2 Timothy 1:7 indicates that God has not given us a spirit of fear, but of power, and of love, and of a sound mind – we must operate in the same spirit using our sound mind, using the power

God gave us through faith and courage
in him and his word, to put it simply we
have to understand who we are in Christ
and what manner of spirit we are of.

Unless were blind, living cave or have
been in a coma or are completely
unaware of anything going on around you
it's pretty clear to see as a born-again
believer in Christ that the rise of the
militant LGBT movement is concentrated
on destroying American Christian values
embedded long ago by the founders of
this nation. They understand that if
America falls the rest of the nations will
also fall. What do they seek – love, peace,
and harmony? I think if you're Christian
and you believe that the Militant LGBT
movement only seeks love, peace, and
harmony that you are either pretty naïve,
willfully ignorant, or greatly deceived. It is
apparent to anyone with eyes to see, ears
to hear, and a heart perceive God's will
that there is a deeper purpose behind the
militant LGBT movement in that purpose
at its core centers on destroying the
things that God has created.

Just look at it for a minute, the family, our children, our societies, and even our churches. Quite frankly the list to go on and on – there is no part of our lives that the militant LGBT community has not attempted to corrupt, destroy, circumvent, or redefine in some way. Is this not truly lawlessness in America and throughout the world.

Now according to my research there is no centralized organization that has control over the entire militant LGBT community or the movement. This is either a very strategic move or a complete lie. I gather it's a little of both, meaning this – there is no way on "Earth" that the militant LGBT movement would be able to accomplish all that it accomplished, and continues to accomplish without a centralized organizational and operational framework. At some given point in my humble opinion there has to be a centralized organizational framework for operations in every facet of our lives to be affected.

Here's the thing, even when the United States was at war with North Korea and was engaged in battle against Chinese troops these Chinese troops despite not having the traditional hierarchy of chain of command still were given orders regarding what the mission was and how to accomplish. This strategy puts the burden of responsibility on each and every member of the Communist Chinese troops seeking victory against the United States Army. Again remember, they still were given orders from those at the top. This seems to be the same strategy that the militant LGBT movement is using but the question is who is at the top?

Now as a mention just a bit ago, there is no way on earth that the Militant LGBT movement could accomplish all that they have accomplished so far without a centralized organizational and operational framework.

If you think that a bunch of militant LGBT anarchist who burn with the lust for one another have the capability and discipline apart from a spiritual backer, a spiritual force if you would could accomplish what they have accomplished sadly you are mistaken. The first time we read about sexual immorality in the Bible that I can recall is when the fallen Angels came down and had sex not just with the women but also with men and other beast of the field. Now I'm sure this may sound a little off to you but nevertheless I would highly encourage you to read books on the subject by author Steve Quayle was done extensive research in this area.

So now it becomes clearer, at its roots lawlessness in America and throughout the world did not even begin on earth but began long ago with a rebellion by Lucifer and his fallen Angels. And this war continues even to this day and the militant rise of the LGBT movement is just one tool that the enemy uses to attempt destroy all that God is created that is holy and righteous and pure.

Brothers and sisters I'm asking you right now to stand with me against the forces of darkness that are destroying our nation, that are destroying our minds, our hearts, our children's future, our very nation. We must do all that we can do and leave nothing but blood, sweat, and tears on the battlefield. What does the Bible say; it says you have not yet resisted sin onto blood – what does that mean to you?

HISTORY OF THE LGBT MOMENT

The LGBT rainbow movement is a collection of groups that represents the rights of lesbian, gay, bisexual, and transgender individuals commonly known in LGBT social circles. This movement originated from Northern California, but nowadays it has operations worldwide. Interestingly enough there is something else up in Northern California the Bohemian Grove. For those that don't know what the Bohemian Grove is let me clarify briefly.

The Bohemian Grove is where once a year leaders from around the world gather, create policy, have orgies of all kinds, and participate in occult rituals. There is a lot of witchcraft and satanic things that take place during this gathering. For a great documentary on the Bohemian Grove check out Alex Jones's film, "Dark Secrets Inside The Bohemian Grove".

In 1978 its core symbol, the rainbow flag was designed by an artist from San Francisco known as Gilbert Baker, and from then its design has undergone several revisions. By 2008, the flag consisted of six stripes; red, orange, yellow, green, blue, and violet; like a natural rainbow. One has to ask themselves why a rainbow and why six colors? Some of you reading this book may know and understand already that God used a Rainbow as a sign of His promise that He would never destroy the earth again through water. Yep heard right the Militant LBGT movements use a sign of God's promises and invert it to mean something unholy.

At its core this is exactly what the Militant LGBT movement wants to do in our societies – but more importantly in our hearts. If everything is acceptable then God's Word will not be tolerated and in fact will become "hate speech". See the deeper roots yet? Its really an attack on God, the Word of God, and All that would follow them – Sounds exactly like what the devil would do right?

RAINBOW COLORS AS AN EMBLEM OF LGBT PRIDE

Today, the rainbow flag has found several applications on all manner of products being sold worldwide including clothing, jewelry and other personal items. The rainbow flag colors are consistently used to showcase LGBT identity and camaraderie. At the present time, the rainbow colors are universally recognized as a symbol of LGBT pride and distinctiveness.

A common item sold by this movement, jewelry, is a LGBT pride necklace or freedom rings that consist of six colored rings, one of each rainbow color, on a chain. My question to all of this is where is the "Churches" response to all of this? Where is Your Personal Response to All of this? Did God's Epistles get lost in the mail, or did you receive them and simply write return to sender on them before giving them back? What have You done oh person of faith?

PUBLIC OPINION

Different societies have different attitudes towards homosexuality that vary greatly in different historical periods and different cultures; there is also a variation on attitudes toward sexual activity, desire and sexual relationships in general. Different cultures have different norms concerning what is deemed as appropriate or inappropriate sexuality; while other sanction same-sex relationships and sexuality, others do not condone such activities.

However, we must look unto God's Word for clarification. What does God's Word say? The Bible declares that the Word of God remains the same regardless of societal, cultural, or historical periods of time. "Heaven and Earth will pass away but God's Word will by no means pass away" (Matt. 24:35). The bottom line here is God's Word is not to conform to our culture, ethnic background, or even us in any way. If we truly want to understand God's standards and do His will we must all come to the simple realization that we must conform to the Word of God, not the other way around.

Religious Opposition Further Illustrates the Lawlessness

Many religions not just the Christian Faith oppose the practices of the Militant LGBT community and do not condone the practices indicated in 50 Shades of Grey.

Some of these other religions include many Abrahamic faiths, the Eastern faiths, Catholicism, Orthodox Judaism, Mormonism and Islam, which hold to the stance that homosexuality is a sin and that its acceptance and practice in any society weakens its ethical standards as well as offends God. Brethren in Christ, we need to contemplate on who we are in Christ so that we will act like it in the right manner, according to His will. A person may claim to be a child of God, however, to act like one is a totally different concept all together. "If we live in the Spirit, let us also walk in the Spirit" (Galatians 5:25). Furthermore, the Scriptures declare, "Wherefore by their fruits ye shall know them" (Matt. 7:20).

CIRCUMVENTING THE RULE OF LAW

Let's now discuss the Supreme Court of the United States ruling regarding seam sex unions. It's kind of funny almost, yet sad at the same time regarding the stupidity of the American people.

Again we must look at what the law says, yes our all famous, and much hated (at least by the left) Constitution of the United States of America. The Constitution United States of America clearly defines the United States Congress as the branch of the government that will create laws for the people – it's just that simple, nothing complex about it, the United States Congress makes the law – period. Again the United States Supreme Court is being used as a tool to circumvent law and the will of the people. The executive branch is now a de facto dictatorship with the use of executive orders, once again to circumvent the will of the people and benefit a powerful global elite. The Supreme Court of the United States job, it's only job, is supposed to be to give their opinion, a ruling if you would on if a law (key word being law here) is constitutional; meaning is it a legal and binding law according to the Constitution of the United States of America. The United States Supreme Court cannot confirm, affirm, or make a ruling on a nonexistent law.

However, nowadays it's clear to see that repeatedly the United States Supreme Court and the executive branch both circumvent the will of the people and the rule of law through their actions. It's important at this point to understand that governors, sheriffs, and civil workers like those in Kentucky who bravely stood up against the tyranny of the militant LGBT movement are under no obligation to make adjustments or accommodations for the militant LGBT community who wish to get married as it were regardless of state law. Unfortunately all too often the United States of America citizens neglect their duty to learn the Constitution United States and guard our nation against any form of enemy both foreign or domestic weather takes the shape of socialism, communism, fascism or combination thereof. I won't even begin in this particular book to get into the radical Islamic agenda or how they are working in coordination with the militant LGBT movement.

Is very interesting to see how anarchist, communist, socialist, and fascist are all working together to bring down United States of America through various means – was MacArthur right back in the day? Again we have to understand that LGBT movement much like the other groups mentioned above have been weaponized – not only physically as it were but also spiritually, to destroy the things, the very foundations in which we exist as a species that God created for us.

The concept of marriage historically, Biblically, or even within nature via procreation has always been between a male and female yet somehow the Supreme Court of the United States of America in all its wisdom, those black robed terrorist as they were described on the Hagmann and Hagmann radio show a while back felt somehow that they were entitled to create a law and most of the general public because of the mass media fell victim to the lie that same-sex marriage is now legal in all 50 states. This is not the case; the Supreme Court of the

United States did not and cannot create any law according to the supreme law of the land the Constitution of the United States of America. If it's supposed to be legal in all 50 states I would encourage every single person reading this book to pull up the law that the United States Congress voted on to create and the Supreme Court ruled on – I guarantee you will not find because it does not exist.

Is there any wonder why United States government in general at the national level has such a low approval rating right now? It's very clear to see regardless of your religious background or lack thereof that the United States government and the politicians running the system are corrupt to the core. Though I'm not a fan by any means of Bernie Sanders it's clear to see that even those on the left that may agree with the militant LGBT community's beliefs are sick and tired of corrupt government and politicians who do not care about the will of the people.

Now again, no politician, especially no one politician, not even Donald Trump will be able to fix this country because at its core this country's problem is a heart problem. The heart of the nation is not turned towards God it is turned towards the things of this world and the pleasures there in. And while we are talking about the executive branch it's important to understand as a born-again believer in Christ that you should not be looking to any other king except the King of kings and the Lord of lords Jesus Christ to solve any and all problems.

This is one of the problems that we face here in America, and throughout the world quite frankly, too often Christians are looking for political solutions to spiritual problems, they are looking to men and not to God, they're looking at each other and not to God – is there any question as to why we are in the shape that were in when we don't look to God Almighty to solve our problems. You don't need to look to any other source

He is the Alpha, He is the Omega, He is the first, He is the last, He is all that you will ever need, and He will provide according to His will – we have a responsibility to stand in the gap, to occupy until He returns and to be the light until His return - but if you hide your light, if you're barely shining yourself, how can you give light to this dark, dying, and corrupt world?

This world right now needs your light; it needs the Spirit of God dwelling within you to proclaim the Word of God boldly, without fear, without reservation, to the ends of the earth in any and every way possible. It truly is a war and there are several battles taking place simultaneously throughout the world – what does the Scripture say, "The harvest is plentiful but the laborers are few". It's time to put down the remote, to step away from your computer, and to focus on the things that matter most and "Take action for the kingdom of God".

Again what does the Scripture say,
"Seek the kingdom of God first and His
righteousness and all these things will be
added on to you". It's time to seek the
kingdom of God first, seek the will of God
first, seek the leading and the guiding of
the Holy Spirit first – it's time to read His
Word on a daily basis, it's time to pray on
a daily basis's, it's time my brothers and
sisters to walk in the Spirit of God with
boldness and conviction through faith and
courage to complete God's will for your
life and if God would grant it restore this
nation's moral compass through changing
the hearts and minds of those around us.

Quite honestly, without this kind of
dedication lawlessness in America and
the world will continue as you sit idly by
doing nothing - commit yourself to battle
and join the fight, get on your knees right
now and repent for sitting idly by and
watching your country go to hell, ask God
to lead you and guide you as to what to do
next, and He will.

THE INDIVIDUAL STATES

By legalizing same-sex "marriages," several states have become official and active promoters of this immoral theme. Some of these States call on public officials to officiate at the "new civil ceremonies", some States have also put out orders that public schools have to teach 'same sex "marriage"' acceptability to the children; another sad thing to contemplate is that there are certain States that may also punish any state employee who expresses disapproval of this subject matter.

Formerly, Massachusetts was the first U.S State to establish marriage licensing for homosexual partners, and that was is in 2004. Ever since then, sixteen States have joined Massachusetts by making the same decision.

As a matter of fact, six 'confused' States made their decisions through the courts, believe it or not, eight of them made their decisions through the State legislature, and worst of all this was the 3 States that made their decision by popular vote; which seems much like the 'Sodom and Gomorrah' of our times. The federal government currently recognizes gay "marriage" for their purposes. In the near future, more states may be forced to make decisions about this matter, or the decisions will be made for them.

And just like so many other situations where marriage directly affects society, the State will anticipate Christians and all people of benevolence to be disloyal to their consciences by overlooking, through silence or deeds, an attack on the natural order and Biblical Truth. It is my hope that you will not be one of these Christians that back down from the fight!

IT ATTEMPTS TO DESTROY NATURAL LAW

Marriage is not like any other relationship between two human beings. It is governed by natural law because it is rooted in the very beginning of creation. And like any other Natural law, it's most basic principle is that "upright morals should be executed or pursued, and evil ones must be shunned." Due to this innate reasoning, people have the ability to perceive what is morally upright and what is not. In addition, people know the results or purpose of each action they take – at least to some degree. Any occurrence that establishes the circumvention of the rationale of the sexual act violates Natural law.

Being ingrained in human nature, natural law is first and foremost universal and it is also immutable. It applies to all human races, with equal dimension. It decrees and outlaws unswervingly, everywhere and all the time. Paul taught in the Epistle to the Romans, revealing that natural law is inscribed on the heart of every man.

"For when the Gentiles, which have not the law, do by nature the things contained in the law, these, having not the law, are a law unto themselves. Which shew the work of the law written in their hearts, their conscience also bearing witness, and their thoughts the mean while accusing or else excusing one another ;) (Romans 2:14-15)

IT AUTHENTICATES AND ENDORSES A LAWLESS LIFESTYLE

The Militant LGBT movement serves to validate not only such unions but it also advocates for the whole homosexual lifestyle not to forget all its bisexual and transgender variants. Apart from Christian Laws, civil laws are used to structure the principles of a person's life in any given society. They play a very vital and often decisive role in manipulating patterns of beliefs, opinions and behavior in mankind. They presumably mold the existence of any society.

However, they also tremendously moderate the public's assessment and appraisal of forms of behavior. Fellow Christians, these are evil men who are controlled by the devil, consciously or not. (Proverbs 12:12,) states, "The wicked disireth the net of evil men: but the root of the righteous yieldeth fruit." We have to take a stand and take personal responsibility for our own actions.

IT MISREPRESENTS AN IMMORAL ACT AS A CIVIL RIGHT

The Militant LGBT advocates argue that same-sex "marriage" is an issue that deals with human civil rights just like the struggle for racial equality that occurred in the 1960s in the United States of America.

Yet another lie to further their agenda and create lawlessness in America! It should not be surprising, after all the devil after all is the father of lies, so it should not surprise you that those who follow him operate in a similar fashion.

A Civil Right is only protected based off of something you cannot change such as your race, national background, etc. Immoral behaviors that people choose to engage in and then attempt to have protected under the law creates a special interest group or class of people if you would with greater protection under the law then the average citizen. The fabrication that an immoral act is a civil right is quiet ridiculous at its core to any person who is still about to connect to their conscious - race and sexual preference are fundamentally contrasting realities. When a man wants to marry a woman the difference in their characteristics, be it race, wealth etc. will not defy law of nature because the two individuals are of different gender, and therefore the necessities of nature are respected.

Same-sex "marriages" will forever oppose nature. There is no way two individuals of the same gender, regardless of race, wealth or stature, will be able to procreate.

There is just a lot of overwhelming biological impossibilities opposing these kinds of union. Another thing to consider is that, genetically inherited and permanent racial traits cannot be compared with behavior that is changeable and more so non-genetic.

EFFECTS ON THE SOCIETY

Taking into account that these schemes go against the basic principles of the Bible, it is our mandate as Christians to deal with this threat that is rapidly destroying our culture and society in order to remove the risks that they pose to future generations. Paul tells us that we are the ambassadors for Christ (II Corinthians 5:20). An ambassador is a delegate sent who is usually sent to represent a ruler to another. Our ruler is Jesus Christ. And our home is in heaven; however, we are His earthly representatives.

The Spirit of the Lord Jesus Christ, living in us, is greater than the enemy in the world (I John 4:4). Also as an assurance, God always causes us to triumph in Christ (II Corinthians 2:14). As faithful ambassadors of Christ it is our duty to lead the battle against these attacks to our way of life – Duties are ours, Results are up to God.

IT'S UP TO THE CHRISTIAN TO HELP RESTORE ORDER

The Book of Leviticus says it clearly, "Thou shalt not lie with mankind, as with womankind: it is abomination." (Leviticus 18:22) prohibits man to lie with mankind as with womankind. It goes on to state that it is an abomination, a disgraceful act. Also in the Old Testament, the story of Sodom and Gomorrah is a clear representation of how God deals with the sin of the Militant LGBT communities. In no way is this acceptable to God – Period!

However, God requires each one of us to do what we can do when we can do it. God is not the God of excuses, but solutions and He has given His Holy Spirit to us so we can accomplish all that He wills for our lives. We have to be brave enough, bold enough, yes haven enough faith to believe His Word and walk His will out. It's up to every born again believer out there to help restore order in our personal lives, our family, our community, and in the Spirit.

TERMINOLOGY

Why do I use the term militant when describing the LGBT community or movement? Apart from a particular group within the movement classifying themselves as such I use the term because of their aggressive, non-accepting, intolerant, strategic warlike behavior.

A great example of this type of behavior was in Kentucky where local civil servant refused to issue a marriage license to a homosexual couple because it violated state law. Now of course this couple came in with the local media and others sympathetic to the cause of the homosexual's couple's situation. If you can still find video on YouTube and other venues of the situation you can clearly see that it was an ambush, there was such hostility towards this civil servant that I'm very surprised that violence of some kind did not break out. In fact it was very reminiscent of Sodom and Gomorrah when the city was outside of lots door demanding that Lot send out to the mob the messengers of God so that they could have their way with them, it was that same spirit, that same depravity that was clearly evident in Kentucky. Yet thankfully the Salt and Light Brigade as well as other Christians rallied in defense both physically and spiritually for the civil servant and her family.

48

For those of you who have not heard of the Salt and Light Brigade I encourage you to search them out online and join with them as it is a great organization. The American Christian Defense Alliance, Inc. supports any Christian organization that is attempting to turn the tides in the hearts and the minds of the people back to Jesus Christ.

Acceptance, Tolerance, and Equality – yeah right, not from the Militant Tyrannical LGBT movement. For as much as they wish to be accepted, for people to be tolerant of their way of life, and to have equality as they put it – they are none of these things. In fact they operate with the same spirit of resentment which leads to hatred that the devil himself has towards God. And as you know a rebellion broke out in heaven and the devil and his angels were cast down for there was no room found for them any longer in heaven.

Now ask yourself this question, what is a rebellion? Is it not war? It is the same rebellious spirit that moves in their hearts to do as they wish with no regard for anyone else that causes them to war against anything and everything that stand in the way of them accomplishing their goals and this is why I use the term militant when describing the LGBT movement.

FURTHER EXAMPLES OF LAWLESSNESS IN AMERICA

Whether you're civil servant, wedding cake maker or someone famous like Kirk Schilling or Joan Rivers it seems no ones safe nowadays from this inverted reality in which the politically correct police will come after you. We have seen this time and time again in America the Militant LGBT movement going after anyone that stands in their way, systematically destroying the foundations of our society.

It's clear to see what their tactics are, some of the tactics include lawsuits, pressuring companies to fire people, or potentially outright killing people in the case of Joan Rivers. Now I say potentially here because that's just speculation, coincidence – but oh is it ever such a coincidence that Joan Rivers would come out publicly and mentioned that Michelle Obama is a tranny meaning a transgender and that Barack Hussein Obama is a homosexual. I find it very much a coincidence that she wines up dead very shortly after these comments were made.

Any man of God out there who supports ESPN or any major sports at this point should really evaluate themselves and understand what they're doing. You may be doing this in ignorance, not realizing the depth of the manipulation and financial backing of the Militant LGBT movement. However, let me make it very clear to you ESPN is owned by Disney and Disney is one of the fundamental places that actively support, promote, and finance the Militant LGBT movement.

As of this writing, April 30, 2016 there is a movement underway to boycott all Target stores because of their gender-neutral bathrooms. This movement was started by the American Family Association and then picked up by other Christian organizations including the Salt and Light Brigade headed up by Coach Dave. Yet if this particular movement is going to be successful than it should include Disney, ESPN, and any other business or organization that supports any way the Militant rise of the LGBT movement.

A GLIMMER OF HOPE?

There is a small glimmer of hope on the physical battlefield as states and governors start exercising their legal authority North and South Carolina are good example of just that. Both states recently enacted laws regarding gender-neutral bathrooms. Thankfully these laws come down on the side of common sense and biblical truth.

Yet the outcry and hysteria from the militant LGBT movement may cause these states to reverse their current laws, only time will tell. As the news of these lost spread throughout the militant LGBT movement several singers and companies have withdrawn from investing their time and energy and money into the states – they are in effect boycotting both North and South Carolina because of their biblical common sense laws. I would encourage every Christian out there that is aware of this to stand with North and South Carolina in prayer and if possible through supporting local businesses in their communities that are known to be Christian businesses.

CHAPTER 2: GOD'S STANDARDS

WORD OF GOD ON: HOMOSEXUALITY, LUST OF THE FLESH, FORNICATION, AND ADULTERY & SELF GRATIFICATION

Fellow Brethren, coming soon is a day when everyone will be required to give an account of our actions here on earth to our Lord Jesus Christ. Paul wrote to the Christians in Rome, saying, "So then every one of us shall give account of himself to God." (Romans 14:12) This means that all unbelievers, liars, those who are fearful, the sexually immoral individuals and so many unruly people will be thrown into the Lake of Flames. This is clearly revealed to us in the Bible, "But the fearful, and unbelieving, and the abominable, and murderers, and whoremongers, and sorcerers, and idolaters, and all liars, shall have their part in the lake which burneth with fire and brimstone: which is the second death." (Revelation 21:8)

I don't know, but perhaps everyone, including you and me, has defied the will of God and joined or promoted these factions in their life. However, as a Christian, what really matters is repentance. Through repentance, your sins are washed clean by Jesus Christ. When we turn away from our sinful natures and repent, He will wash us clean. The most intriguing thing about Jesus Christ is that He will cleanse us so many times as we learn to rely on Him and overcome our sinful nature. However, there are some people who love to sin, in addition, they don't want repent. These are the type of people who are bound to come under this dreadful condemnation during judgment day. God cannot be mocked whatever a person sows that to they will reap.

As a believer who has repented of your sins, it doesn't stop there, there's still an evaluation that you continue to make of our life and actions – are they in the faith?

If your actions are not in the faith and your realize you have sinned - this might not result in eternal destruction but it will definitely result in some kind of loss. All the dealings that we undertook, that were not done in submission to the Word of God will be burned up. There's no reward for all the things that we did out of our own meager human inventiveness, independent of God. Don't look back and regret the time you wasted serving the lust of the flesh.1 Corinthians 3:15 states, "If any man's work shall be burned, he shall suffer loss: but he himself shall be saved; yet so as by fire."

A common problem that so many of us have is that we do not want to assess our way of living to see if it is in accordance with the standards of the Almighty God. Must of us would rather do the evaluation of other Christians and focus on them instead of looking inward and reflecting to see the true status of our heart.

When we see other Christians buying a copy of 50 shades of grey, or joining the LGBT movement, do they also give us temptation of some kind? Perhaps it's because we imagine that there is something cool that we are missing, or we want to go with the flow and be popular, or maybe even more sinister we wish to escape tribulation, persecution, or slander and believe that there is safety in the numbers of other Christians doing the same thing. Nowadays, so many Christians are taken by the paradigms of this world, while they are at it; they end up neglecting some, if not all of the things that matter and that God deems as important. They try their best to be consistent with the worldly standard of beautifying outward appearance, however, when you put up with the presence of all manner of repulsive attitudes like prayerlessness and selfishness, in a subtle way you are promoting bad behavior. Remember, God always sees the inside motives of your heart.

God Almighty is and will always provide for and protect individuals who fear Him and most of all those who tremble at the mentioning of His Word. He highly esteems people who fear Him in addition to those who hate evil ways. The Lord says, "Thus saith the Lord, The heaven is my throne, and the earth is my footstool: where is the house that ye build unto me? And where is the place of my rest? For all those things hath mine hand made, and all those things have been, saith the Lord: but to this man will I look, even to him that is poor and of a contrite spirit, and trembleth at my word." (Isaiah 66:1-2)

In the end, our actions will be ascertained by the principles of the Word of the Lord. As much as we may have accepted Jesus Christ, do we also strive to carry on in His Word? Do we renounce the lusts of this world on a daily basis so that we can truly love our God and also relay that love to others? Do we affectionately seek devoted communion with our God in prayer more than we read the daily morning newspaper or check our email?

Do we take care of the widows and orphans around us, the poor and hungry in our societies, or those who are in prison? God will no doubt judge accordingly on Judgment Day - did these things matter most to you while you were yet alive? We need to seek God to help us honor His standards, even if it means not conforming to the measures or expectations of human success that the world would have us measure success by.

WORD OF GOD ON: HOMOSEXUALITY, LUST OF THE FLESH, FORNICATION, ADULATORY & SELF GRATIFICATION

Nowadays, there are so many guys, including Christians, who follow a vague understanding of "love," some of whom condone the homosexual practice. They usually do this without realizing that the "love" that is described in the Bible absolutely excludes homosexuality because of its sinfulness.

As Christians, we can best share the gospel of our Lord Jesus Christ with homosexuals through walking in love, true love that the Bible describes and speaking with compassion, knowing that we too once walked in darkness and were condemned not knowing Jesus or walking in His ways. The Militant LGBT community already understands their sin, describing what the really is to them according to the Bible will only inflame them further to rebel against a loving God who wants all men to be saved and come to the knowledge of the truth (2 Thessalonians 2:4). If you take a good look in some chapters in the Bible, particularly Genesis 1–2, Matthew 19, and Ephesians 5; these passages clearly describe the way God has instituted marriage; a heterosexual, faithful relationship where the two become one. When humans decide to go against the Law of God, they are actually eroding their human purity through practicing immorality.

This is clearly illustrated in the Chapters of Genesis 19, Jude 7, and also in 2 Peter 2. These practices also devastate the divine foundation of marriage. In the Books of Leviticus 18 and 20 and also in Romans 1, God's instructions are laid out quite clearly concerning the repulsiveness of homosexuality in His sight. That being said, even we as Christians, there none who hasn't fall short of the Glory of God. In the Books of Isaiah 56 and 1 Corinthians chapter 6, we can see that God being full of MERCY has a plan for homosexuals; just like many sinners, they need to find freedom and forgiveness through a life-changing faith in His only Son, Jesus. The door is wide open for people who practice same sex relationships to accept God's invitation.

Today, immorality is perhaps this generation's favorite surrogate for love. The Apostle Paul uses the Greek word 'porneia' to refer to all kinds of illicit sexual sin.

Popular culture and trends that people these days want to adhere to, desperately try to blur the line between immoral passion and genuine love. But any act of immorality is a total perversion of genuine love; it violates both the first Commandment (Mark 12:29-30) by disobeying God's Word when you decide not to love Him, and the Second Great Commandment (Mark 12:31) In addition to this when you go ahead and seek self gratification rather than the spiritual good and sanctification of others then you are also committing a sin (Rom 13:9-10.)

Impurity; another mischievous sprite that attempts to pervert true love is also discussed by Paul in the several epistles of the New Testament. He uses the Greek term 'akatharsia', to refer to all kinds of filth and impurity in this world, particularly peculiar characteristics of evil companionship such as, "filthiness," "foolish talk," and "crude joking." This kind of companionship has nothing to do with true love; Paul plainly says that this trait has no place in the Christian's way of life.

Another attempt to corrupt love, Covetousness, stems from an egotistical desire for self-gratification. This particular trait is the exact opposite of what Christ set as an example when He "gave up His life for us."

As Christians, in order to show authentic love to the people who embrace and advertise these movements, we need to openly and courageously speak the truth about these perversions of love with a spirit of compassion for our fellow man's soul. Most people who talk about love these days ignore its basic principles. Most individuals try to redefine "Love" as having a broad tolerance, overlooking sin while embracing good and evil in the same measure. However, this is not love; God's love is not like that. The Scripture vividly explains the love of God in terms of propitiation, sacrifice and atonement for sin: "In this is love, not that we have loved God but that He loved us and sent His Son to be the propitiation for our sins" (1 John 4:10).

To put it simply, Jesus Christ offered Himself as a sacrifice in order to turn away the wrath of an offended holy, righteous, and just God. In order to dismiss our sins, God, with love, gave His Son as an offering for our sins. God did this to satisfy His own wrath and justify all who believe in Jesus Christ.

In other words, true love is always merciful, sacrificial, sympathetic, self-giving, compassionate, generous, kind, and patient. The Scriptures associate true love with so many positive, benevolent qualities (1 Corinthians 13:4-8.)

But we cannot overlook the negative side as well, in Ephesians 5 it explains more about the person who truly loves others like Christ; that he does must refuse every kind of counterfeit love. In the passage, Paul, names some of these worldly forgeries. These aspects are what corrupt our societies to embrace such vile movements.

They include - immorality, impurity, and covetousness. He also goes on to further say, "But fornication, and all uncleanness, or covetousness, let it not be once named among you, as becometh saints; Neither filthiness, nor foolish talking, nor jesting, which are not convenient: but rather giving of thanks. For this ye know, that no whoremonger, nor unclean person, nor covetous man, who is an idolater, hath any inheritance in the kingdom of Christ and of God. Let no man deceive you with vain words: for because of these things cometh the wrath of God upon the children of disobedience. Be not ye therefore partakers with them."

THE LOVING TRUTH ABOUT LGBT LIFESTYLE

As a Christian, you need to shun away the ways of the world. Do not at any point in your life; allow ungodly acquaintances not even family members to persuade you to sin!

Considering that true love demands us to have courage as Christians to confront false love and its fruits, acts of homosexuality must be graciously yet purposefully condemned. It is a sin. Even though the Militant LGBT moment advocates for this act, terming their motivation as love, the Bible clearly notes such passions and attractions as counterfeit love and a perversion. It is immorality, impurity, covetousness, and lust that fuel the Militant LGBT's desire. Also the conduct that results from this desire is disgraceful to even speak about. The truth about the acts of the Militant LGBT community, as depicted from the Scriptures in the Bible, is that it is neither a natural nor a normal act; certainly it is not morally neutral. Instead, it is a pervasion of God's created order; a violation of His revealed will—causing it to be extremely sinful as it is bizarre and disgraceful.

In addition, so-called Christians who develop a tolerant attitude toward the LGBT lifestyle, citing "true love", are for a fact exhibiting anything but true or divine love. Those Churches whose leaders defend homosexuality, while affirming gay and lesbian ministers degrade God's moral standard; they also lead others to sin. Since when did condoning sin have a part in true love? Authentic love always encourages people to do the right thing and should not be used as an excuse for wickedness. "By this we know that we love the children of God, when we love God, and keep his commandments. For this is the love of God, that we keep his commandments: and his commandments are not grievous."(1 John 5:2–3). Loving Christ means that we have to obey Him (John 14:15); on the other hand loving other people is to encourage them to do the same (Heb 10:24). When we decide to take a Compassionate but firm action of speaking the truth to unsaved sinners, this is the basic meaning of loving the lost with a true love.

Unless or until a sinner recognizes their sin, they will not see their need for a Savior; not understanding the fact that they are under the wrath of God. Until they cry out for mercy and put their trust in Jesus Christ, they cannot be saved. We need to show and advice sinners about their current guilt before God and the future condemnation that awaits them if they decide not to repent.

If we truly want to reach out to the Militant LGBT community then we need to start using the gospel as our armour, we as Christians must begin by letting them know about God's Word on homosexuality; an abomination in the eyes of the Lord. There's no single occasion when the Bible ever condones homosexual behavior on any level. To be more precise, it consistently condemns this type of lifestyle choice and indicates that God hates it as well as promises to punish all those who do not repent and leave this abominable way of life.

Unless those of the Militant LGBT moment comprehend that the lifestyle that they are trying to promote is inherently and unnaturally sinful, at no point will they ever desire to seek the forgiveness that has been offered to them by God and decided to forsake their iniquity and embrace our Lord Jesus Christ.

WHAT THE BIBLE SAYS ABOUT HOMOSEXUALITY?

On the matters concerning homosexuality, God's Word is neither ambiguous nor silent. Unfortunately, the contemporary church has been deeply blinded through the issuance of pro-homosexual literature, advocacy and on a deeper level a demonic spirit of deception. Those that classify themselves as Pro-homosexual Christians who exist in our societies, assert that the order that has been made in the Bible are either too vague or too ancient to remain relevant in our times.

But that's not the real issue here, the real matter, as with most moral compromises in many modern churches, is a love of sin; an idolatrous craving for international cultural acceptance, diversified with an arrogant contempt for the Word of God by laughing demons who continue to pervert the truth. The truth of the matter still remains that homosexuality has never been affirmed by God's Word, His people throughout history, the Israelites, nor the church. But, the contemporary Christian church has done little more than blur the waters with unnecessary ambiguity and controversy. The good thing about the Scriptures is that God's Word directly talks about homosexuality in both the Old and New Testaments; and in doing so; it has already established a divine outline for proper human sexuality. The Bible has provided divine illustrations of God's wrath against sexual perversion; it has set forth divine instruction that has directly prohibited homosexuality. In spite of that, it has also significantly offered a divine invitation for sinners to redeem themselves of their sins through repentance and embracing Jesus Christ in faith.

WHAT DOES THE BIBLE SAY ABOUT FORNICATION?

This is a serious topic where many people including Christians totally disregard what God says by accomplishing their own will. Every day, we hear about so-called Christians who are also fornicators. Currently, around the world, there is so much pressure for people to engage in premarital sex, the government also seems to encourage this through the issuance of contraceptives in educational centers. However, true Christians need to remember that we have been set apart from the world; we are no longer of this world. Any Christian who rebels against the Word of God is not a Christian at all.

FORNICATION AND ADULTERY

On almost a daily basis, you will not fail to hear about Christians who are also fornicators.

In our times, where there is a lot of pressure on the populous to indulge themselves in premarital sexual activities, as a Christian you ought to remember that you were set apart from the world and its earthly things, you have the Holy spirit to guide your actions on earth. If you are the kind of Christian who rebels against God's Word, then you may want to consider if you are a Christian to begin with.

When you are tempted by the devil to indulge in acts of fornication, he will never let you know about the benefits of waiting until the day that you get to marry your spouse to have sex. The devil will always be a liar, and his lies will go down with him in the eternal lake of fire. In other words, do not let other people's opinions influence your decisions on this matter. So many people in the world love fornication; you might be one of these people. But you need to ask yourself, is it a Godly act to embrace or encourage? Is it the right thing to do? What does the Bible say about fornication? And lastly is it the safest thing to do?

Focusing your thoughts on God and not on the needs of the flesh will ultimately save you from shame, death, guilt, unwanted pregnancies, STD's or even false love. In addition, you will also be given God's exceptional blessing in marriage just to mention a few.

To avoid fornication you need to shun away peer pressure from the world around you and renew your mind with the Word of God. You also need to seek guidance from the Holy Spirit in order for you to make appropriate life choices starting this day. And on matters of copulation, you've got to be trustworthy and faithful to your spouse, whom you've married. If you are not yet married you have to maintain abstinence from acts of fornication because when you fornicate you sin against your own body, which is the Temple of God. Lastly for all youth who think they cannot abstain it would be advisable to get married and then start building your family with the grace of the Almighty God rather than to burn with the passion within you.

WHAT THE BIBLE SAYS ABOUT FORNICATION!

1 Corinthians 6:13-14 says, "Meats for the belly, and the belly for meats: but God shall destroy both it and them. Now the body is not for fornication, but for the Lord; and the Lord for the body. And God hath both raised up the Lord, and will also raise up us by his own power."

1 Thessalonians 4:3-4 "For this is the will of God, even your sanctification, that ye should abstain from fornication: That every one of you should know how to possess his vessel in sanctification and honour;"

1 Corinthians 6:18-19 "Flee fornication. Every sin that a man doeth is without the body; but he that committeth fornication sinneth against his own body. What? know ye not that your body is the temple of the Holy Ghost which is in you, which ye have of God, and ye are not your own?"

1 Corinthians 5:9-11 "I wrote unto you in an epistle not to company with fornicators: Yet not altogether with the fornicators of this world, or with the covetous, or extortioners, or with idolaters; for then must ye needs go out of the world. But now I have written unto you not to keep company, if any man that is called a brother be a fornicator, or covetous, or an idolater, or a railer, or a drunkard, or an extortioner; with such an one no not to eat."

WHAT THE BIBLE SAYS ABOUT ADULTERY!

Proverbs 6:32-35 "But whoso committeth adultery with a woman lacketh understanding: he that doeth it destroyeth his own soul. A wound and dishonor shall he get; and his reproach shall not be wiped away. For jealousy is the rage of a man: therefore he will not spare in the day of vengeance. He will not regard any ransom; neither will he rest content, though thou givest many gifts."

Deuteronomy 22:22 "If a man be found lying with a woman married to an husband, then they shall both of them die, both the man that lay with the woman, and the woman: so shalt thou put away evil from Israel."

Proverbs 1:15 "My son, walk not thou in the way with them; refrain thy foot from their path:"

Romans 12:2 "And be not conformed to this world: but be ye transformed by the renewing of your mind, that ye may prove what is that good, and acceptable, and perfect, will of God."

SELF GRATIFICATION

Fellow Christians, sexual immorality also includes lustful sin and self-gratification. This is because these are not in accord with the word of God. As a Christian, you need to think about this keenly!

If you indulge yourself in this manner, you are carrying out a premeditated sin, reason being, you always have to think about executing the act before you actually do it! If you want to stop, then you must willfully resolutely stop with the grace and mercy of the Lord Jesus Christ.

BIBLE VERSES ON SELF-GRATIFICATION

Galatians 5:16-26 - I say then, Walk in the Spirit, and ye shall not fulfill the lust of the flesh.

Acts 8:22 - Repent therefore of this thy wickedness, and pray God, if perhaps the thought of thine heart may be forgiven thee

Romans 12:1 - I beseech you therefore, brethren, by the mercies of God, that ye present your bodies a living sacrifice, holy, acceptable unto God, which is your reasonable service

Hebrews 13:4 - Marriage is honorable in all, and the bed undefiled: but whoremongers and adulterers God will judge.

1 John 2:16 - For all that [is] in the world, the lust of the flesh, and the lust of the eyes, and the pride of life, is not of the Father, but is of the world.

1 Peter 2:11 - Dearly beloved, I beseech you as strangers and pilgrims, abstain from fleshly lusts, which war against the soul;

REMINDERS TO THE CHRISTIAN CHURCH

Jude 1:4 "For there are certain men crept in unawares, who were before of old ordained to this condemnation, ungodly men, turning the grace of our God into lasciviousness, and denying the only Lord God, and our Lord Jesus Christ."

1 John 2:3-4 "And hereby we do know that we know him, if we keep his commandments. He that saith, I know him, and keepeth not his commandments, is a liar, and the truth is not in him."

WARNING TO THE CHRISTIAN CHURCH

Jude 1:7-8 "Even as Sodom and Gomorrah, and the cities about them in like manner, giving themselves over to fornication, and going after strange flesh, are set forth for an example, suffering the vengeance of eternal fire. Likewise also these filthy dreamers defile the flesh, despise dominion, and speak evil of dignities."

1 Corinthians 6:9 "Know ye not that the unrighteous shall not inherit the kingdom of God? Be not deceived: neither fornicators, nor idolaters, nor adulterers, nor effeminate, nor abusers of themselves with mankind." Revelation 22:15 "For without are dogs, and sorcerers, and whoremongers, and murderers, and

idolaters, and whosoever loveth and maketh a lie."

MESSAGE FROM GOD'S LAW: BE HOLY!

And the Lord spake unto Moses, saying, Speak unto all the congregation of the children of Israel, and say unto them, Ye shall be holy: for I the Lord your God am holy. Ye shall fear every man his mother, and his father, and keep my Sabbaths: I am the Lord your God. Turn ye not unto idols, nor make to yourselves molten gods: I am the Lord your God. (Leviticus 19:1-4)

When considering any aspect from the law of God, there are certain questions that you need to ask yourself. What is the message being relayed? Is it really possible to summarize the law of our Almighty God?

In the Bible context illustrated above, the Lord only mentions a few of His commandments from His holy law. He talks about proper treatment of parents, How we should observe the Sabbath day by keeping it holy, and abstaining from idolatry. In summary, He provides a two-word summation of all His law: "be holy."

Through this calling of holiness, God wants holiness to be a distinctive trait in us; nonetheless, what is the holiness of the Almighty God? It obviously has something to do with His character. In the Lord, there is perfect righteousness. In God, there dwells no unrighteousness. In Him, abides total moral purity. Conversely, in our God, there is not even a single trace of evil moral fiber. Our God is in fact, morally unpolluted and spiritually pure.

This trait of holiness of our Lord defines the standards of how we should live or lives; the law, which holds forth for human race. Israel, God's chosen nation, was given this Law in writing. Others have this Law written in the conscience (Romans 2:15). Since we are born into this world, we are governed by God's law; the Law itself demands a holy character from us in Christ, including how we relate to our Creator and also how we relate to each other.

Chapter 3: True Love Waits

True love lasts

Exodus 20:6 talks more about God's love to mankind. It says, "And showing mercy unto thousands of them that love me, and keep my commandments." This verse relays the lasting love that God has towards His people; if they do not waver in His Law. Also this particular feature is true for relationships, particularly marriage. Spouses who actually love each other in reality often tend to bear with each other's shortcomings by taking into account youthful connections, whether positive or negative, and also future expectations. Even though this process may prove to be difficult, it should be observed in order to develop true love and also so that the love between the spouses lasts.

TRUE LOVE COMES NATURALLY

True love cannot be replicated, in other words it is pure. A good example of natural love can be seen between a child and his or her parent. In John 14:15 Jesus says, "If ye loves me, keep my commandments." As Christians, our natural love in the Word of God develops as we continue to obey and follow the commandments of God. In verse 23 Jesus further explains, " Jesus answered and said unto him, if a man love me: and he that loveth me shall be loved of my Father, and I will love him, and will manifest myself to him."

TRUE LOVE IS NOT DEMANDING

Leviticus 19:18, while talking to Moses, God was stipulating Laws to Govern His chosen people, He stated, " Thou shalt not avenge, nor bear any grudge against the children of thy people, but thou shalt love thy neighbor as thyself: I am the LORD."

The reasoning behind this feature is that if you love someone, you should not plan to harm them even if your neighbor has done something to you; rather you should love them. By doing this not only will you be following the Law of Almighty God, but, you will also set a good example for others to follow. If you Love your neighbor as yourself, then you should not expect them to change through force, so that they can fit into your principles, the best way to go about it is to pray first and then try to initiate dialogue. Alternatively you should be able to accept each other's weaknesses in order to build up real love. Try to view your homosexual neighbor as one who is overcome with the plans of the devil, pray for him or her before trying to initiate a dialogue, but keep in mind that if you don't love the person in the first place then it is pointless.

Like so many things in this world, commitment relies on one's patience virtue. Through commitment one is able to be in love with the Creator and His Laws, with their genuine partner who is before them, instead of other fantasies, dreams or masters of this world. What you need to resolve to commit yourself to at this moment is the word of God. In Mathew 6:24, Jesus teaches us more about love and commitment. He says, "No man can serve two masters: for either he will hate the one, and love the other; or else he will hold to the one, and despise the other. Ye cannot serve God and mammon." All that you truly have is what you have here at this moment, so it bodes well to focus on that, at the end of the day, it is shrewd to give your full consideration and your affection to that. You cannot serve God and at the same time look for excessive (gross) wealth and material avarice. This scripture is also referred in Luke 6:13

LOVING STRANGERS AND ENEMIES OF THE SPIRITUAL WORLD

People who practice most of the negative things that we have discussed earlier are of this world. However, we as Christians, are not of this world; therefore we are strangers to them of the world the same way we view people who love this world as strangers of the word of God and its spirituality. So many times you will find yourself having difficulties coping with the behaviors of that troublesome 'stranger' who is living next to you, whenever you are able to learn how to cope and be fond of them, you will be taking a step further to discovering the meaning and effectiveness of true love. Leviticus 19:34 says, "But the stranger that dwelleth with you, and thou shalt love him as thyself; for ye were strangers in the land of Egypt: I am the LORD your God.

These sentiments are repeated in Deuteronomy 10:9, "Love ye therefore the stranger: for ye were strangers in the land of Egypt." Mathew 5:43-44 also talks about loving your enemies (in this case, our enemies are all those who do not love or support the Word of God. The Jesus says, "Ye have heard that it hath been said, Thou shalt love thy neighbor, and hate thine enemy. But I say unto you, Love your enemies, bless them that curse you, do good to them that hate you, and pray for them which despitefully use you, and persecute you;" Jesus further explains the reason for loving your enemies in verse 46, stating this, "For if ye love them which love you, what reward have ye? do not even the publicans the same?" This scripture is also referred in Luke 6:32, 34.

To conclude this matter is a verse from the scriptures from our Lord Jesus Christ. In John 15:13, He says, "Greater love hath no man than this, that a man lay down his life for his friends." If you love you neighbor and you do not want to lose him or her to the devil, then you need to help the person even if it means that you end up losing your life in the process.

TRUE LOVE WAITS

Everybody says it's OK, but you know it's not. You might even be mocked by your friends for being a virgin, but you know it is the right thing to do. In a time where sex is nothing but a casual "activity" between individuals, staying a virgin until marriage seems like an impossible feat. But, let me tell you this: God is pleased when you save yourself until marriage because that's the exactly how he designed sex to be. Sex should only be between a married couple, Genesis 2:24 tells us "Therefore shall a man leave his father and his mother, and shall cleave unto his wife: and they shall be one flesh."

Unfortunately, the world has twisted the meaning of sex. Sex nowadays is something that people casually do. The hard truth is, some people have sex just for the sake of it, and not because they love each other. Some have sex with the same gender, and others, or multiple partners. The world's definition of sex is such a great defiance of God's beautiful gift to a husband and wife.

WAITING FOR LOVE

Now that we have laid God's true purpose
for intercourse, I hope you fully
understand how important saving
yourself until marriage is so important,
especially to God, our Father. The apostle
Paul wrote in 1 Corinthians 6:18-19, "Flee
from fornication. Every sin that a man
doeth is without the body; but he that
commmiteth fornication sinneth against
his own body. What? Know ye not that
your body is the temple of the Holy Ghost
which is in you, which ye have of God, and
ye are not your own? For ye are bought
with a price: therefore glorify God in your
body, and in your spirit, which are God's."
The question now is, what then should
you do now that you're still young and
aren't ready for marriage yet?

 When we fill our minds with God's Word,
we have nothing else to focus on but His
Word. "But seek ye first the kingdom of
God, and His righteousness; and all these
things shall be added unto you." Matthew
6:33

GOD'S PURPOSE FOR SEX

REPRODUCTION

This is quite one of the most obvious purposes of sex between married couples. After God had created man, male and female (Genesis 1:27), He then blessed them and charged them with a command, "...Be fruitful and multiply, and replenish the earth, and subdue it: and have dominion over the fish of the sea, and over the fowl of the air, and over every living thing that moveth upon the earth." In the further chapters of the book of Genesis, you can see God instituting two holy institutions, which are marriage and family.

This again, obviously tells us that God's charge for us to procreate should be within the holy institution of marriage between a male and a female; He wants children to be conceived and born in a family.

Many actually abuse this, believing that sex is a way of expressing their affection for a person whom they love, even outside of marriage. Yet, we go back to our Biblical understanding that sex should only be between a married male and female. In Ephesians 5:25-31, Paul reminds us that the purpose of marriage and becoming one flesh (sex) is love.

"Husbands, love your wives, even as Christ also loved the church, and gave Himself for it…(v.28) So ought men to love their wives as their own bodies. He that loveth his wife loveth himself. For no man ever yet hated his own flesh; but nourisheth and cherisheth it, even as the Lord the church… (v.31) For this cause shall a man leave his father and mother, and shall be joined unto his wife, they two shall be one flesh."

PLEASURE

This might surprise you, as you may feel that having pleasure in sex with your spouse is unbecoming of a Christian. But you have to understand that man is also designed by God to give pleasure and to receive pleasure as well. In fact, you can also see an entire book of the Bible (Song of Solomon) that is about the sensual and romantic love that is shared between a man and a woman, and you can see in Song of Solomon 2:10-13 about a man's invitation to a woman to be his partner in pleasure.

However, you have to keep in mind that pleasure in sex is only a part of a marriage. Being married together also means having pleasure with waking up beside each other every day, watching the sunset go down, and hearing your children's laughter. Yes, sex is also for pleasure, but it is only to be enjoyed by a man and a woman within their marriage.

BOUNDING

Another purpose for sex is for two individuals, husband and wife, to be bonded together as one. Remember, marriage is designed for two lives to be as one in serving and glorify God. And to be united with each other, couples should get to know each other in a deeper sense.

Genesis 4:1 tells us, "...Adam knew Eve his wife; and she conceived, and bore Cain, and said, I have gotten a man from the Lord." Of course, we know that the word knew, means Adam and Eve, being a married couple, had an intercourse and were blessed to have their first born. But a deeper understanding of this word tells us that Adam not only had sex with his wife, but he also got to bond with her, to get to know her deeply, physically, emotionally, and spiritually.

CHAPTER 4: DEVILS TRAPS

TIME TRAPS

Time Traps, what are Time Traps? A Time Trap can be considered anything that consumes your time. Addictions of any kind would be classified as a time trap. Many people reading this book may be struggling with various addictions to pornography, immoral sexual behavior, or wrestling with the lust of the flesh. Understand you are not alone in the struggles many other fellow believers are also struggling with the same things that you are but it's important to confess your sins before Almighty God for he sees your heart and nose your thoughts – there is nothing hidden that he does not see no matter how you try to hide it.

As a born again Christian believer in Christ you have to guard against time traps, addictions, and any other thing that would steal your time away from what God has called you to do. For many of us as husbands that may actually include your "Honey Do" list. For those that do not know what a honey do list is, it is the list of items that your wife continually has for you most likely just in time for the weekend.

Now many of us may know that old adage, "happy wife, happy life" but let me tell you right now and I don't mean to sound harsh when I say this, but your happiness should not be your primary focus God's will for your life should be your primary focus. You have to remain with your eyes fixed upon him and his word to ever truly fulfill your destiny. If you ever truly want to fulfill your destiny in Christ then you must remove and guard against whatever time traps are in your life and focus on God's will and making yourself available to be used by God.

Some other time traps include television, music, sports, video games, and being in front of your computer all day. Time traps do not necessarily have to deal with the lust of the flesh or pornography of some kind although that too is a time trap. We have to be wiser than this and not just look at one area of our lives as Christians we have to be self-aware and understand the vices that the devil uses to ensnare us. However, the word of God declares, "Greater is he that is in me than he that is in the world" (1 John 4:4). If God has given you a vision for your life you need to get focused and start walking out that vision by removing these hindrances to the call of God on your life – identify them and remove them. We all have them, no one is exempt, just identify them, remove them, and repent of them as you start to truly walk out your destiny through courage and faith in Christ.

MASS MEDIA, TV, MUSIC, PORNOGRAPHY

HOW THE DEVIL USES TELEVISION, MUSIC AND PORNOGRAPHY TO TRAP CHRISTIANS

The power of information is so massive that it can build up a nation and destroy it within the same manner. Now imagine the effects of the damage it causes when used for the wrong purpose by spiritual forces, the principalities of power beyond human capabilities for undirected purpose of snaring Christians.

The devil workers are everywhere, when you think you are safe that is the time you are deeply immersed in his tricks, which are not open to the naked eyes. It requires the spirit and the fruits of the Holy Spirit to constantly dwell in the life of the Christian and to be able to discern the truth from evil, which comes from the devils traps.

The television becomes more interesting to watch when the people you are paying attention to show a littlie skin to catch our attention. The devil is clever, we have to watch and pray continually as Jesus commands, for at the slightest opportunity we may get ensnared if we as Christians forget about the Word of God and its principles. To get ahold of strong men of God, the devil will use woman because men from the beginning with Adam were trapped through Eve.

Show a little skin and skimpy erotic moves are enough to sway the men who are not strong in faith. Once the society is rotten to the core and our foundations are destroyed what can the righteous do? (Psalms 11:3) We can still resist the devil and he will flee – temptation is the same way.

Music is the modern day addiction; even churches are having an absolutely difficult time deciding which songs will be allowed to be played in the church. As Christians the fruits of the Holy Spirit will help us discern between the Godly songs and the evil intentioned songs. The new generation songs that promote drug abuse, fornication, anarchy, rebellion, lust, fighting, murder, rape, violence, drinking and false religion, all originate from the devil. Remember that Lucifer was the lead worship in heaven no wonder he has so much influence over the music industry and knows how to play with the minds of Christians not fully grounded in their faith. You probably have listened to songs that you do not know the meaning of or the true intention of but the superstar behind the ingenious songs know very well what they mean. Some of them have struck a deal with the devil to produce this very captivating addictive music to praise the devil and in return they are given fame and constant flow money.

The term addiction can be explained well by those who love watching pornographic movies; yes it wipes away the spiritual common sense in ones brain. When we are attracted to pornographic material we must realize that there is a serious war going on both internally and in the spiritual realm - the Angles of the Lord Jesus Christ are at war with the principalities of the darkness. But we are given the will to choose what we want but the pleasures of the flesh seem to win all to often. 2 Timothy 2:26 says, "And that they may recover themselves out of the snare of the devil, who are taken captive by him at his will." God burned down the ancient cities of Sodom and Gomorrah which were wiped away in an instant in God's fury. That is how God dislikes all forms of the Militant LGBT community. The wickedness of the Militant LGBT community causes the Lord so much fury and just like those ancient cities, destruction will eventually come our way because we did nothing to stop those engaging this type of behavior.

Ephesians 6:11 states "Put on the whole armour of God, that ye may be able to stand against the wiles of the devil." The brainwashing that this first moving captivating and bounding information have in Christians is massive. The war against the devil can only be won will the help of the Holy Spirit.

Parents be watchful and careful, so that even as you protect your young ones from the devil, you do not become the source and the vehicle through which the devils gets into your family. Prayer is important, remember to read the Word of God and worship Him in Spirit and in Truth. 1 Peter 5:8 that says, "Be sober, be vigilant; because your adversary the devil, as a roaring lion, walketh about, seeking whom he may devour:"

MEN LOVE DARKNESS RATHER THAN LIGHT

John 3:19 – 21, Says, "And this is the condemnation, that light is come into the world, and men loved darkness rather than light because their deeds were evil. (vs. 20) for everyone that do with evil hated the light, neither, to the light, lest his deeds should be reproved. (vs 21) but he that do with truth cometh to the light, that his deeds may be manifest, that they are wrought in God."

Every single one of us have an evil sin nature this is something we must recognize if we are ever to make progress in wage war successfully against our spiritual enemy. Roman 3:10 clearly tells us, "as it is written, there is none righteous, no, not one: there is none that understand, there is none that seek after God." So what do we do with such a sinful nature, and nature contrary to nature of awesome God we serve? The word of God says in Galatians 5:16, " . . . Walk in the spirit, and ye shall not fulfill the lust of the flesh."

Now on your own you could never do this but God gives us away and his way is quite simple. His way is to renew your mind continually with the word of God so you do not conform to the world and all its ways (Rom 12:2 / Eph. 4:23). If we wish to increase our faith, what do we need to do? The Scriptures declare that faith cometh by hearing and hearing the word of God (Rom 10:17). So it's a two-part thing, we need to read and study God's word as well as hear the word of God being preached and preached by people that are anointed of God that truly have the spirit of God not your typical 501C3 churches that have pastors who sell other congregations for monetary gain – but that's a whole separate book in and of itself and I could go on for a while about that topic.

2 Corinthians 5:17 says, "Therefore if any man be in Christ, he is a new creation: old things are passed away; behold all things are becoming new".

How many of us understand the phrase,"
you control your sin?" Yes we all have us
in nature and yes we all will fall short
each and every day but for some believers
in the faith they feel they can exercise
some type of control over their sin and
thus play with fire so to speak. Some
Christians are aware when they are about
to send, they recognize that they are in a
battle with their flesh yet instead of
running directly to God in prayer and
doing battle in the spirit they get a place
for the devil and slowly but surely give
into the lust of the flesh. Normally when
we are faced with overt temptations that
we can clearly identify it's easier to fight
against them because we see them for
what they are and can identify that these
are actually attacks from the wicked one.

However, the lick will always come before the nibble. Now let me back up just a minute and explain what that actually means. As anyone who has ever raised a dog knows, during the time of teething dogs have a habit of trying to bite whatever they can, and nibble here, and nibble there, a nibble everywhere. But what I found out while examining the behavior of my own dog is that my dog would always lick my hand before attempting to nibble on – this the exact same thing that Christians do with sin.

This is what we do whether we recognize it or not? We commit our heart casually to the lick, to test out how this will feel, taste or give pleasure in some kind of way. Then much like Eve, after we see some kind of benefit from it we continue and we nibble and most of the times we continue to nibble and take ever increasing full-sized bites into the Apple we will call sin.

This has to stop my brothers and sisters, we have to identify the precursors to what causes us to sin (our triggers if you would), we have to identify when we are in the lick phase, and this lick phase is the escalation phase in the cycle of sinning. And make no mistake about it there is such a thing as a cycle of sinning. For anyone familiar with crisis intervention and what is known as TCI you could easily replace the different phases of the crisis cycle with words or labels to describe the sinning cycle.

CHAPTER 5:
CONSEQUENCES OF SIN

SCRIPTURE VERSES AND WARNINGS

CONSEQUENCES OF SIN

Like your earthly father, our God and Father in heaven is concerned about our well-being. He of course, wants to give you great things, but like your Dad, God will also allow you to face the consequences of your sin to remind you that you're disobeying Him and to also lead you again to His path.

Remember that our God has many names. He has been called a loving God, a gracious God, an all-knowing God, and He is also a just God. All throughout the Bible, we see God's calling for us to obey Him, and in it, we can also see the consequences of defying Him.

Many people today might not see pre-marital sex as a sin, but this is just like any other "grave" sin; and committing it has serious consequences.

"Know ye not that the unrighteous shall not inherit the kingdom of God? Be not deceived: neither fornicators, nor idolaters, nor adulterers, nor effeminate, nor abusers of themselves with mankind, nor thieves, nor covetous, nor drunkards, nor revilers, nor extortioners, shall inherit the kingdom of God." 1 Corinthians 6:9-10

If you study the Bible diligently, you'll see that there are a lot of verses that shows us the consequences of sin, but what exactly are they?

IT SEPARATES YOU FROM GOD

Isaiah 59:2 makes it clear for us that sins create a separation between us from God. This explains why we seem distant to the Lord whenever we live in sin.

That's why sometimes you'll find it hard to pray, or even go to church when you don't ask for forgiveness from your sins. But don't misunderstand this as God moving away from you when you sin. In fact, God's love covers us even if we're sinners. The only reason why we feel distant from God is because we're the ones that are moving away from Him when we sin.

Remember in Genesis 3, when Adam and Eve fell into sin? Wasn't God the one who looked for them (v.9) after they became afraid and hid from God (v.10)? No, it doesn't mean that God didn't know where they were, but it only shows us that we are the ones who distance ourselves to God when we sin.

Any sin that you repeatedly commit and fail to repent to God leads you to more sin. A "simple" kiss, leads to petting, caressing, and then finally leads to having sex. What seemed harmless in the beginning ended up you finding yourself in deep waters with no way out. This also goes for our imagination. God judges us also according to what we think and it is these thoughts that can be a title wave overflowing and consuming that are the precursor to physical actions that God calls sin. We must guard our hearts and our minds if we want to walk in the Spirit.

Unless you listen to the Holy Spirit convicting you, and repent to God of your sins, you will see yourself committing sin, after sin, after sin and the cycle of sin will continue. "Repent ye therefore, and be converted, that your sins may be blotted out, when the times of refreshing shall come from the presence of the Lord;" Acts 3:19

IT HURTS OTHERS

Don't ever think that sinning only affects you. In fact, sinning also hurts the people who love you and care for you. One pastor's daughter in a local church admitted to her parents that she was pregnant out of wedlock. Of course, this hurt her father a lot. Being a minister, seeing your child fall into sin is like a direct stab to the heart. Of course, God's forgiveness is always there, but this situation not only hurts the parents, but can also lead some of the congregation to stumble. Imagine, if you allow yourself to engage in sexual activity, don't you think you're hurting the people you love because you are putting yourself in a dangerous situation?

Another story from the book of Genesis is found in Chapter 19 where the Lord destroyed the cities of Sodom and Gomorrah. The men in the city were so into sin that God allowed wrath to happen in the city (v.13). The Lord rained down fire and sulfur from the sky to the both cities leaving everything in them to burn to the ground. The story of Noah, also in the book of Genesis (Chapters 6-7), is another example of God allowing destruction (Gen.6:17) through a great flood to wash out the wicked people.

You see, God might not be sending fire to rain down or a great flood, in our time, but this only shows us that we can face destruction whenever we sin and fail to ask God's forgiveness for it both personally and as a nation.

It Can Bring Divorce

Divorce – everyone knows the ridiculous numbers in the divorce rates in the United States of America but how many people know that the numbers are almost identical when compared to those they claim to be Christian? As you can see from the Militant rise of the LGBT movement one of their primary goals is to destroy the family structure God ordained and created. This destruction of the family at its core centers on the destruction of the Biblical concept of marriage. Once the core family structure is destroyed there is little to stop the destruction of our children, and thus the future of our nation.

Marriage is sacred to God and there's only one justifiable way to get a divorce and that is because of sexual immorality according to Jesus. Matthew 5:32 says, "But I say unto you, That whosoever shall put away his wife, saving for the cause of fornication, causeth her to commit adultery: and whosoever shall marry her that is divorced committeth adultery.

" For the Lord Our God hates divorce as Malachi 2:16 writes, "For the Lord God of Israel says That He hates divorce, For it covers one's garment with violence," Says the Lord of hosts. "Therefore take heed to your spirit, That you do not deal treacherously."

IT SENTENCES YOU TO ETERNAL DAMNATION

Romans 6:13 is clear, to tell us that "...the wages of sin is death;" If you're a believer and know what God wants us to do, but disobey Him, you also commit sin (James 4:17).

My prayer is that as a Christian, you won't allow your sins to be unforgiven by God. Yes, it is in our nature to sin, that's why God has allowed Jesus to die on the cross for our sins and in our stead. It is you and I who deserve death because we are sinners, but Christ became the perfect lamb, the sacrifice to wash us from our sins; and I hope that you won't forget that. God's forgiveness is always available; you just have to ask for it.

BIBLICAL EXAMPLES

DAVID AND BATHSHEBA

Some of you may be familiar with the story of David and Bathsheba. However, for those that do not know the story I will summarize it here. Now David was the king of Israel and was at war during the time that he first saw Bathsheba. Bathsheba was a beautiful woman that David seen bathing herself while he was yet in his palace. King David inquired about the woman he saw bathing herself. A messenger returned to him indicating the woman was and that she had a husband who was a soldier for King David. Now David wanted Bathsheba for himself and conspired against her husband sending him to the most fierce part of the battle. Shortly thereafter it was reported to King David that Bathsheba's husband was dead. During this entire time King David dealt treacherously with Bathsheba and her husband and God was not pleased.

God sent Nathan the prophet to King David to inform him of God's deep displeasure and the consequences of his actions. Now when David heard this he was convicted in his heart and spirit and prayed to God for forgiveness. In Psalm 52 we can read his prayer of repentance. However, the child that Bathsheba was caring ended up dying as a direct result of King David's sin.

So because of the lust of the flesh and the desires there in King David sinned against the Lord. What did it cost him, what are the consequences of the sin – a death of a child, faithful soldier dead, but so much more. These actions not only have a direct consequence on those that commit sin but also indirect consequences, unintended consequences if you would. But thankfully King David was a man after God's own heart, he identified, rather he recognized that he had sinned and earnestly sought God's forgiveness praying that he would not take his precious Holy Spirit away from.

The absence of the Holy Spirit, the absence of the living God in your life is the true consequence of sin and King David recognized that fell on his face and repented.

David's Prayer of Repentance

To the Chief Musician. A Psalm of David when Nathan the prophet went to him, after he had gone in to Bathsheba.

51:1 Have mercy upon me, O God, according to thy lovingkindness: according unto the multitude of thy tender mercies blot out my transgressions. (v2) Wash me throughly from mine iniquity, and cleanse me from my sin. (v3) For I acknowledge my transgressions: and my sin is ever before me. (v) 4 Against thee, thee only, have I sinned, and done this evil in thy sight: that thou mightest be justified when thou speakest, and be clear when thou judgest. (v5) Behold, I was shapen in iniquity; and in sin did my mother conceive me. (v6) Behold, thou desirest truth in the inward parts: and in the hidden part thou shalt make me to know wisdom. (v7) Purge me with hyssop, and I shall be clean: wash me, and I shall be whiter than snow. (v8) Make me to hear joy and gladness; that the bones which thou hast broken may rejoice. (v9) Hide thy face from my sins, and blot out all mine iniquities. (v10) Create in me a clean heart, O God; and

renew a right spirit within me. (v11)
Cast me not away from thy presence; and
take not thy holy spirit from me. (v12)
Restore unto me the joy of thy salvation;
and uphold me with thy free spirit. (v13)
Then will I teach transgressors thy ways;
and sinners shall be converted unto thee.
(v14) Deliver me from bloodguiltiness, O
God, thou God of my salvation: and my
tongue shall sing aloud of thy
righteousness. (v15) O Lord, open thou
my lips; and my mouth shall shew forth
thy praise. (v16) For thou desirest not
sacrifice; else would I give it: thou
delightest not in burnt offering. (v17) The
sacrifices of God are a broken spirit: a
broken and a contrite heart, O God, thou
wilt not despise. (v18) Do good in thy
good pleasure unto Zion: build thou the
walls of Jerusalem. (v19) Then shalt thou
be pleased with the sacrifices of
righteousness, with burnt offering and
whole burnt offering: then shall they offer
bullocks upon thine altar.

WOMAN CAUGHT IN ADULTERY - JOHN 8: 1-11

8:1 Jesus went unto the mount of Olives. And early in the morning he came again into the temple, and all the people came unto him; and he sat down, and taught them. And the scribes and Pharisees brought unto him a woman taken in adultery; and when they had set her in the midst, They say unto him, Master, this woman was taken in adultery, in the very act. Now Moses in the law commanded us, that such should be stoned: but what sayest thou? This they said, tempting him, that they might have to accuse him. But Jesus stooped down, and with his finger wrote on the ground, as though he heard them not. So when they continued asking him, he lifted up himself, and said unto them, He that is without sin among you, let him first cast a stone at her. And again he stooped down, and wrote on the ground.

And they which heard it, being convicted by their own conscience, went out one by one, beginning at the eldest, even unto the last: and Jesus was left alone, and the woman standing in the midst. When Jesus had lifted up himself, and saw none but the woman, he said unto her, Woman, where are those thine accusers? hath no man condemned thee? She said, No man, Lord. And Jesus said unto her, Neither do I condemn thee: go, and sin no more.

Now in the story local Pharisees bring a woman caught in the act of adultery, the one and only one way that Jesus claimed that divorce is permitted. Yet look at how Jesus responds to the allegations. Jesus is not looking to condemn anyone but to save everyone through him. The story should offer hope to those that are struggling with the lust of the flesh, wrestling with the lifestyle of the LGBT community, or anything there in between. Jesus Christ does not want to condemn you he wants to show you love but much like the woman in the story, Jesus commands you to "Go and Sin No More".

THE ADVERSE EFFECTS OF 50 SHADES OF GREY

SATANIC RITUALISTIC SEXUAL ABUSE AND MIND CONTROL TECHNIQUES

What's more sickening, this novel even portrays IPV as romantic and passionate. Last year in the Journal of Women's Health, Amy Bonomi, L. Altenburger, and N. Walton published an article on the effect of Fifty Shades of Grey. Their conclusion was quite intuitive and very alarming:

"While intimate partner violence affects 25% of women and damages health, present societal conditions—including the normalization of violence in popular culture such as films, novels, and music—generate the context to support such abuse."

Emotional torture is almost present in nearly every interaction illustrated in this book, including: stalking; intimidation; and isolation. Sexual violence is insidious—especially using alcohol to entice a woman's consent, as well as intimidation, altered identity, and stressful managing. In the book, the lead female role becomes disempowered and ensnared in the relationship as her conduct becomes mechanized to respond to her partner's abuse.

So you still think that the 50 Shades and Militant LGBT moment is just a sexual, self-gratifying moment with no central command structure? Emotion torture is what these demonic forces literally feed off of and this is why those that practice Satanism use ritualistic sexual abuse to invoke this type of trauma, emotional torture and cruelty. This is one way that they create "slaves" who are conditioned not to think, but to respond to key things, which then triggers the desired mechanized response from the victim.

Very few Christians understand the depth of the battle and who and what we are honestly facing. The said part is most are not mature enough in Christ to even step onto the battle field, or worse yet cowards who hide behind the walls of the building that they call a church. Its time to grow up in the Lord my Brothers and Sisters and get yourself in the battle – We need your help Now! Please start praying in earnest for all of us in the fight if you do nothing else.

IT PROMOTES SADISM AND SATANISM

Considering that the book promotes the acts of bondage, domination, sadism, and masochism, it would be repulsive to claim that "affection" or "intimacy" has anything to do with it. We have to also remember our spiritual enemy and his workers use these types of acts in their ritualistic sexual abuse of their victims, especially during their "holy days" like April 19th - May 1st and during October 31st, which ultimately end in human sacrifice after the continued torture.

The definition of sadism is; "the enjoyment one gets, particularly sexual enjoyment, from being cruel or violent from causing pain to someone else," a sexual perversion where satisfaction is obtained by the infliction of mental or physical pain on others. This is a major part of the satanic ritualistic sexual abuse that people continue to think of as no big deal or just some fetish. We have to mature my brothers and sisters and understand the enemies tactics to avoid being ensnared – but even more important know the Word of God.

IT PROMOTES CONSENT AS NOT BEING ABUSIVE

The individuals that support this novel and what it stands fore keep broadcasting this dim-witted notion that just because someone consents to an idea or allows something to take place, that it isn't abusive.

This misconception is dire as it encourages the gruesome acts depicted in these novels to take place; it actually encourages guys, especially the youth to engage in these horrifying acts.

But supposing one consents to being slapped, beaten up, whipped, labeled degrading and disgusting names, and have other sordid things done to them, some of which I cannot even describe here, does that make the act any less vicious or abusive? Despite the fact that it might be legal, it definitely doesn't make it any less violent or disgusting. As a Christian, would you want to see your daughter in such a relationship? Also, would you want your son to turn into someone who does these repugnant acts to ladies?

If you have ever worked with casualties of domestic and sexual assault, you will understand that just because someone permits something to happen, doesn't mean it isn't, in actuality, abuse. The disturbing thing about all this is that, only when it comes to matters of conjugation, do people start making this argument, they do this so that they can stick to their engrossments and justify their fixations.

In addition the women who defend these books on the grounds that it improved their sex life are being exceedingly negligent and egotistic, refusing to reflect about how these books could affect other women who might be in different situations, more so young and vulnerable girls.

IT MISLEADS THE POPULATION THAT ITS JUST FANTASY AND FICTION AND THAT IT HAS NO EFFECT ON THE REAL WORLD!

This notion is total nonsense and the ones promoting the book (Fifty Shades of Grey) and the lifestyle that it endorses know it. This book is just an explosion of acquiescence for people to try something new, dangerous and quite appalling in their bedrooms. Keep the marriage bed pure brothers and sisters (Hebrews 13:4). There's an old saying, "The greatest trick the devil ever did was convincing the world he didn't exist" – It's not just a fantasy Saints of God, it's a real life battle.

IT DEMEANS THE VALUE OF WOMEN AND GIRLS

What does sadism or sexual abuse, consensual or not, express to our culture concerning the value of girls? What does it express to our boys regarding how they should treat girls?

The youth of today are snowed under with porn and other sexually violent material. As a Christian, are you not at all worried about the impact these materials have on them? What about the girls who get abused by boys who consider that this is normal conduct, and believe it is normal themselves?

Books like Fifty Shades of Grey and the sadism that they promote are offensive on human dignity, and most of all distasteful to the value and worth of girls and women. As a Christian, please consider the impact that it'll have on your daughters, the vulnerable and confused people around you when you decide to read or promote these books. Keep in mind that the lead female role in this book is, thankfully, a fictional character. However, real girls are facing these demands and expectations from a culture that exalts a sexual sadist to the status of a romantic hero.

IT HAS DENIED CHILDREN EITHER A FATHER NOR A MOTHER

For any child's best interests, he or she needs to be brought up under the influence of his or her natural parents (father and mother.) This judgment is substantiated by the manifest difficulties being faced by many children who are orphans or are nurtured by single parents, relatives, or foster parents.

This regrettable state of affairs affecting these children will be the new norm for all children nurtured under a same-sex "marriage." It's just common sense, children raised under same-sex "nuptials" will always be robbed of the affection or tenderness that they should get from either the natural mother or father. These kids will inevitably be fostered by one party that realistically has no blood relationship with the child – then what?

These children will without a doubt be deprived of either a mother or a father to look up to as a role model. In summary of this point Same-sex "marriage" has lead to the disregard of children's' best interests.

THIS UNIFICATION HAS CREATED NATURALLY STERILE UNIONS AND NOT FAMILIES

Unlike traditional marriages, those who normally frustrate its true purpose, do violence to the natural order of things disrupting the balance in the force so to speak by preventing the birth of children through the means of contraceptives called same-sex "unions" which are inherently sterile and useless. Whenever the "partners" want a child, they usually have to elude nature through artificial and costly means; some also go to the extents of employing surrogates.

IT OFFENDS GOD

This is the last and most serious effect that this movement has brought about. Natural moral order was established by God, and whenever one sins or offends what God took His time to build, there will always be consequences. This is what Same-sex "marriages" are doing. Accordingly, as Christians, because we profess to love God, we must be opposed to it.

Marriage was established by God, and there's a reason why our first parents were Adam and Eve and not 'Gilbert and Harvey' or 'Judy and Lisa'. In the Bible, (Genesis 1:27-28,) states, "So God created man in His own image; in the image of God created him; male and female. And God blessed them, and God said unto them, be fruitful, and multiply, and replenish the earth, and subdue it..."

This same concept was taught by Our Savior, Jesus Christ in the book of (Mark 10:6-7,) it reads, "But from the beginning of the creation God made them male and female. For this cause a man shall leave his father and mother; and shall cleave to his wife;"

Lastly as we contemplate on the adverse effects brought by these nefarious groups, let's not forget the teachings in Genesis where God punished Sodom and Gomorrah for the sins of homosexuality, (Genesis 19:24-25.)

Chapter 6: Protect Your Marriage

Guard your eyes

I hate the summer because of the lack of clothing people wear. It becomes much more challenging not to glimpse upon something inappropriate, compelling or desirable in such a way yet we must do our best to guard her eyes to better train our bodies to be in submission to the Spirit of God to war against the lust of our own flesh. Yet the heat of the summer has an equal competitor striving for the hearts and minds and souls of people all around us – the TV and the Internet. It all starts with a glimpse to spark a desire – it is truly a snowball effect and this is why we have to guard what we see.

It's true that in this generation, falling into temptation is easier compared to decades ago.

Today, as early as you hit puberty, you might notice your peers are already engaged in sexual activities, having sex is already a norm. Pornography isn't now only limited to magazines or adults films, now, you can see naked people on the internet, music videos, or posing for photos wearing almost nothing, and you see mainstream movies and TV series with lots of sexy scenes.

The Scripture is full of warnings to help us avoid falling into sin and you can also see plenty of God's promises to those who avoid it. The Bible is our sword to help us fight temptation, Ephesians 6:11 says, "Put on the whole armor of God, that ye may be able to stand against the wiles of the devil."

Don't put yourself in compromising situations

Even though you feel that you know how to stand your ground and are able to turn away from temptation when it comes, it would be better if you do not allow yourself to be close to the invitation to sin. Remember that the devil works hard to make Christians fall into sin. Being alone with a date in your home may seem harmless, but this is definitely one example of you putting yourself in a situation where you will be tempted to fall into sin.

"Watch ye therefore, and pray always, that ye may be accounted worthy to escape all these things that shall come to pass, and to stand before the Son of man." Luke 21:36

Not putting yourself in compromising situations is one of the best ways to avoid issues that may potentially arise and protect your marriage accordingly. If you are married man or woman there is no reason in the world why you should be alone with the opposite sex at any given point in time, you are inviting temptation into your life when you do that or at least the parameters for temptation to take place. All too often married couples go throughout the day casually with no real thought about protecting their marriage or placing themselves in compromising situations that leaves an open door for temptation and sin.

Now this applies to the workplace, and applies to the church, it applies to every area of your life never put yourself in a situation in which you are alone with the opposite sex or for that matter have a best friend of the opposite sex. Your best friend should be your spouse know what else.

Now I shouldn't have to say it but considering the state of our union, and state of people's hearts it's important to note also here that going out with the guys are going out with the girls should be avoided at all cost. If you are married that situation should no longer exist for you. If you wish to go out you should do so with your spouse.

BE AWARE AND DON'T PREPARE FOR SIN – BE PREPARED TO DO GOD'S WILL

It's important to know yourself and to know your weaknesses, your temptations, and your triggers for s sinning. Being self-aware cannot be overstated here, in the military they have a term called situational awareness as Christians we need to have something similar I call it spiritual situational awareness. And for those that aren't familiar with the term situational awareness is just what it sounds like being aware of your complete and total situation on a continual basis my term includes the spiritual realm and thus the addition of the word spiritual.

Now being aware is one thing but don't consciously prepare for sin. There is nothing we can do regarding what we are doing on a subconscious level to prepare for sin but if you're aware, if you have that situational awareness that I just discussed you will be conscious about the things that you're doing and you will not actively prepare for sin. To gain this level of spiritual situational awareness requires reading God's word, hearing God's word, praying, and being right with God.

Just as important as it is not to prepare for sin it's also equally as important to prepare to do God's will. For in doing this you neutralize any subconscious preparations you made for sin because you are actively consciously preparing to do God's will on a continual basis. You may be asking yourself how do I prepare to do God's will? Well that honestly depends on what God's will for you truly is. If God is put on your heart to see the homeless are hungry for example it would be important to have food in your vehicle as drive-by those that are in need.

However, regarding your marriage you could do random acts of kindness that are spontaneous – flowers are always a winner. While random acts of kindness and love may be appreciated it's important to go well beyond that and plan time together that is special to both of you in some way.

PRAY FOR AND WITH YOUR SPOUSE

Another great way to protect your marriage is to actively pray together. It's pretty hard to sin against your spouse when you're actively praying together on a consistent basis. Now that's not to say that there are people out there who have a heart of stone and won't be tempted to do whatever it is that they want to do to begin with yet for the majority of people this will go a long way to increasing their spiritual situational awareness and convict them of sin or potential sin. So when was the last time you prayed with your spouse?

Remember one of the primary goals of the militant LGBT movement is to destroy what God is created and brought together and that includes your marriage. If you haven't started praying with your spouse encourage you to start the process.

If your spouse is not a believer in the Lord Jesus Christ than its important even more so to keep your spouse in prayer to keep yourself in prayer as the Lord may do a work in both of you and give you a testimony to share with those around you.

FELLOWSHIP WITH BELIEVERS OF THE SAME SEX OR IN COUPLES

Fellowship with people or couples who share the same faith, like the people in your church, who will help you avoid temptation. Help each other to walk a deeper spiritual walk with Jesus. Share your struggles and ask for prayers.

However, seek guidance from mature Christians who will guide you and help you overcome what you're facing not immature Christians new to the faith or very young. Also remember not to forsake the gathering of yourselves together with other believers as the time of Jesus return draws ever closer.

"He that walketh with wise men shall be wise: but a companion of fools shall be destroyed." Proverbs 13:20

CHAPTER 7: YOU ARE THE TREASURE

When you're attempting to overcoming 50 shades of grey and all the colors of the Militant LGBT rainbow you have to remember one important thing God made you special and unique for His purpose. No matter how many people tell you that you are not and no matter how many flaws that you have, in God's eyes (and in your parents' eyes), you are special and born with a divine purpose for such a time as this. Like I said a couple of times earlier, as a believer of Christ you have become a part of God's family (Galatians 3:26). This means that you are a princess because you are the daughter of the Kings of Kings, so don't allow yourself to be treated any lesser for any reason.

The world tells us that it's OK to go out and make yourself available to whomever, but you have to know that you are more precious than that.

Keep in mind, that you are the treasure so don't go out looking for love—you have to allow the treasure hunters to look for you and God will send them to you in His time. God's will for you is to connect with someone whom you will end up marrying (1 Corinthians 7:1-3). He doesn't want you to go out on several dates with different people to find the one that's perfect for you, He wants you to patiently wait for His timing and to allow His will to unfold in your life.

Psalm 37:4 tells us to "Delight thyself also in the Lord: and He shall give thee the desires of thine heart" This means that when we find delight in serving God, reading His Word, and following His commands, He will bless us with what we're praying for according to His will. In this context, He will lead you to the person He created perfectly for you. You don't have to make yourself available and be in a treasure hunt to look for the right person, God wants you to be the treasure and He wants you to wait.

Now, this may seem exasperating to you, especially if you see your friends and everyone around you already involved in some type of relationship and engaging in lustful desires. But let me tell you this, waiting for God's perfect timing means that He is preparing you for something great. "How precious also are thy thoughts unto me, O God! How great is the sum of them!" Psalm 139-17

IF YOU START TO BECOME FRUSTRATED WAITING FOR GOD TO GIVE YOU THE "PERFECT ONE", ALLOW YOURSELF TO REMEMBER THESE THINGS:

GOD HAS A GREAT PLAN FOR YOUR LIFE

His will may not fall in line with yours, but remember that His plan is always the best. Even before you were born, God already knew everything about you (Psalm 139), He knows what you need, and He has your best interest in mind all the time.

Jeremiah 29:11 says, "For I know the thoughts that I think toward you, saith the Lord, thoughts of peace, and not of evil, to give you an expected end." Our God is a loving merciful God who wants peace for your life, yet we might have to endure tribulation to finally see it God doesn't have evil in His heart towards us and desires to give us a future and a hope in Jesus Christ. This future and hope is only possible through Jesus Christ and without Him we can never hope to have any reasonable future that includes peace. We must submit to Him completely as best we can in sincerity and truth. God right now, this very moment is calling you to repentance, submission, and obedience to unlock the keys to your destiny – And make no mistake about it each one of us has a God given destiny that the devil is trying to destroy with so many distractions. Stay Focused.

GOD IS PREPARING YOU FOR GREATER THINGS

Don't ever think that there's nothing happening when you're praying and waiting on the Lord. In fact, when you wait on God, you start to be anxious on something, so that when His time comes and your prayer answered, you come to appreciate more what He has given you.

GOD IS BUILDING YOUR PATIENCE

Praying and waiting on God builds your patience not only to wait on the perfect person for you, but He is also preparing you to wait for bigger things that He wants to accomplish through you. "Wait on the Lord: be of good courage, and He shall strengthen thine heart: wait, I say, on the Lord." Psalm 27:14

GOD IS TRANSFORMING YOUR CHARACTER

By waiting on God's timing and trusting His will, you are allowing the Lord also transform you completely so that you will be ready when the one you're praying for comes in your life. "Knowing this, that the trying of your faith worketh patience. But let patience have her perfect work, that ye may be perfect and entire, wanting nothing." James 1:3-4

TRUST ONLY IN HIM

Finally, praying and waiting on the Lord for the person you will marry also teaches you to trust God alone. You don't have to put yourself out there; because you know the He will make a way for you to end up with the person He just created for you. Don't be too anxious when praying for the right person to come, if it's according to God's will, then they will surely come.

Do not allow yourself to be pressured with the people who are around you – Stand strong in Christ and put on the full armour of God. Finally my brothers and sisters fill your heart and mind with God's word and delight in His promises for He alone will direct your path onto perfection.

Chapter 8: You Set The Standard

If you are younger remember even before your parents allow you to enter into the process of courtship, there might be several people who will show interest in you. However, it is up to you whether you reject or accept the advances of these people and overcome 50 shades of grey and all the colors of the Militant LGBT rainbow. If you're a Christian, you must understand that dating several people or "experimenting" with partners, for the sake of having a special someone in your life to feel "loved", or satisfying your physical needs, without the intent of ending up in marriage is not God's way but the worlds.

Your Father in heaven, and your parents here on earth doesn't want you to be in a relationship that will hurt you, that's why your parents would want you to enter into a process of courtship when you're mature enough. So you don't have to go around and test the waters by dating before you can say that you're ready for marriage.

As we all know, the Bible clearly instructs us not be equally yoked with unbelievers, but what else do you need to look for in your future spouse? What do you need to pray for when asking God for the right person to come in your life in the future?

SOME STANDARDS OF COURTSHIP

MY FUTURE SPOUSE SHOULD BE A SERVANT OF GOD

How a person looks, how fit are they, and how they carry their clothes should be the least of your concerns when setting the standards for the ideal person for you. More than their physical features, one of the top most criteria that you should pray for is that your future spouse should be a servant of the Lord. Several verses in the Bible tell us that we should serve God, and also serve others as an act of worshipping the Lord, and this is one thing that you should look for in your future partner in life. When a person wants to court you, look at where they spend most of their time. Do they serve in the church? Are they involved in a ministry? Do they find joy in serving others? All things to consider when looking at the future and protecting your marriage from 50 shades of grey and all the colors of the Militant LGBT rainbow.

MY FUTURE SPOUSE HAS RESPECT FOR ME

Another criteria that you may want to consider is for a person who truly respects you to be the one God sends you. Remember you are the treasure not the treasure hunter. Its important to speak up and tell your potential spouse about your vow of saving yourself until marriage. Afterwards they will be the one who should take the initiative to respect your boundaries, if not then they most likely are not the one God has sent to you. There's no need for you to argue with them if you don't want physical contact during the process of courtship because they respect you and care too much about you if in fact they truly respect you. Your future spouse must love you like he loves himself (Ephesians 5:28-29).

MY FUTURE SPOUSE HAS EYES ONLY FOR ME

As soon as you start getting to know someone, you will already know whether they are serious about pursuing a courtship if and when they keep their eyes only on you. Even if more attract people, or rather people who you feel are better looking than you pass by, they won't allow their eyes to wander, because they respect you. They will also avoid situations that will put them closer to temptation, not only because they love you, but they are willing to follow God's command (Proverbs 4:23-25).

MY FUTURE SPOUSE HAS GOALS AND IS AMBITIONS FOR SERVING GOD

You know that a person will be a perfect spouse when they have ambitions and are actively seeking God's plan for their life. When you're married, you are to submit (if you are the wife) (Ephesians 5:22-23) yourself to your husband, that's why you want to look out for a person who knows how to steer their life through God's guidance.

MY FUTURE SPOUSE GLORIFIES GOD

It will be so easy for some people to brag about their accomplishments when they don't have Christ in their lives. Of course, you don't want to be with someone who focuses on themselves rather than caring for you and for others. You want your future spouse to be good and yet, self-less. Find a mind that acknowledges that their accomplishments, their talents, and everything that is in their life comes from God. That it is the Lord that enables them to do such things.

MY FUTURE SPOUSE LOVES GOD ABOVE ALL ELSE

This might be hard to understand for non-believers, but as Christians, you should want a person who loves God above you and everything else.

This type of person will treat you far better than a person who is just focused on loving you. This person willfully follows God's commands, will serve you, will love you, will be faithful to you and will give themselves for you just as Jesus did for us and just as God has commanded.

These standards might seem an impossible feat, but remember that God only wants the best for you. He wants you to be with someone who will not only pass your standards, but pass His standards as well because He wants you to have a healthy and loving relationship—a type of relationship that can stand as a testimony to others and will reflect all the glory to His name. A relationship that is covered by the Blood of the Lamb and White as Snow.

CHAPTER 9: RESPECT YOURSELF

RESPECT AND PROFESS YOUR BELIEFS

Even if you get rejected, and even if it means turning down the people who would like to ask you on a date. God is pleased when you let other people know your commitment to sexual purity. A person who won't respect this only means that they don't deserve to be a part of your life. Don't be afraid to commit to this and to stand firm on this, for this is what God wants you to do. Wait on true love; wait on the Lord, for He has promised good things to his children who obey.

"Therefore, my beloved brethren, be ye steadfast, unmovable, always bounding in the work of the Lord, forasmuch as ye know that your labor is not in vain in the Lord." 1 Corinthians 15:58

JUST BE YOU

Maybe at a young age you've already encountered people who made you feel that you are less then they are because you do not support the Militant LGBT moment. Or maybe you're too focused on your internal battles with the lust of the flesh and that's why often times you feel bad about yourself. Because of these things, you might have either tried your hardest to win other people's approval or you sulk and hate yourself because you're not able to win your battles and are consumed by the lust of the flesh. But let me tell you this, even if other people make you feel bad, or even if you have a ton sins, God still loves you! No one can do it on their own we all need to take it to God in prayer and understand you are a Child of the Most High – Respect yourself for you are indeed royalty.

If you're familiar with the story of creation in the book of Genesis, after God has created day and night, the heavens, the land and waters, the plants and the animals, He created man. And no, He didn't just create man out of nothing; He created man in His own image and likeness, "So God created man in His own image; in the image of God He created Him; male and female He created them." Genesis 1:27, this means, you are special! If you read God's word, you will see that there a lot of verses that tell you how important you are in God's eyes. One verse that reminds us about this is Deuteronomy 7:6 that says, "For thou art an holy people unto the Lord thy God: the Lord thy God hath chosen thee to be a special people unto Himself, above all people that are upon the face of the earth."

BUT HOW COME A LOT OF PEOPLE TRY TO CHANGE THEIR APPEARANCE, WHICH WAS MADE IN GOD'S IMAGE AND LIKENESS?

Maybe because they want to fit in, they want to impress the people they like, and gain more attraction. However, I tell you now that you will not find true happiness when you focus on these things; you have to respect yourself by honoring how God made you. Furthermore, It is only when you focus on God's love for you and accept Jesus Christ as your savoir that you will find true joy. This is the joy that goes beyond any physical sensations of immoral acts of sin. This is the joy that makes you respect yourself and embrace the gifts that God has given you.

What I'm talking about is the respect that focuses on being thankful for what God has made and what He has blessed you with.

If you want to earn respect from other people, and probably attract a person you're interested in, then you must also start loving and respecting God first. Stop changing yourself just so you can fit into what most people perceive as "beautiful" or "attractive". God uniquely designed each of us with spiritual gifts (1 Corinthians 12:1-11), and we are to use them to bring honor and glory to Jesus Christ. When we embrace these gifts, we allow ourselves to directly follow God's will in our lives, and through it we will be immensely blessed.

If you've been feeling lowly about yourself because of other people's mockery, or you have been hating yourself because you questioned your physical attractiveness, what you need to do is to start forgiving others and forgiving yourself as well. Don't allow the bondage of bitterness; rejection, and self-hatred hinder you from seeing the beauty of what God has blessed you with.

The Lord gave us a commandment to love others as we love ourselves (Mark 12:31) and it would be impossible to do that if you don't respect and love God first. Instead of wallowing in self-pity and wishing you were more attractive and beautiful, focus on praising God because He made you. "I will praise thee; for I am fearfully and wonderfully made: marvelous are thy works; and that my soul knoweth right well. "Psalm 139:14

CHAPTER 10: TEMPTATIONS

It's quite wrong to think that when you become a Christian, you will be immune from facing temptations. Do you think the devil is lurking around unbelievers to get them off course? Of course not! They are already of the world and disobeying God. Satan's schemes are in fact focused on Christians who are attempting to do God's will; to cause them to stumble and fall into the snare of sin.

In Matthew 4:1-11, we can see the story of Jesus being tempted by the devil in the wilderness. After forty days and forty nights of prayer and fasting the devil dared to tempt Jesus not once, but three times in exchange for all "good things" that the devil has promised Christ. But how did our Lord Jesus respond to these temptations? He responded to the devil by saying that "man shall not live on bread alone," but on God's word, that the Lord should not be put into the test, and that man should only "worship the Lord your God, and serve Him only."

Another words He responded with the Word of God. We should learn from Jesus and respond to temptations that come our way in like manner.

Maybe you've already experienced being tempted in the past. In our time when our culture has been highly sexualized and having intercourse out of marriage has become a norm, it's quite difficult not to fall into sin and to keep yourself pure until your marriage. You see, it's actually normal to feel tempted about these things; however, it is how you respond to them that actually counts. When Jesus was tempted by the devil it was His response that made the difference.

The Bible also reminds us to be vigilant against falling into temptation: "Be sober, be vigilant; because your adversary the devil, as a roaring lion, walketh about, seeking whom he may devour" (1 Peter 5:8). That's why even before temptation would come your way, it would be wise if you have already shielded yourself from sin with the Shield of Faith.

MOVE YOUR FOCUS AWAY FROM SEXUALITY

It's true that man and woman were created as sexual beings. In fact, one of the first commands of God to man is to "be fruitful and multiply, and replenish the earth, and subdue it;" That's why it will be inevitable for humans not to be sexually attracted to another person. But, you also have to remind yourself that this command from God was made only for a married man and woman.

You may encounter some situations where you will become sexually attracted to someone, but you must learn to turn away from this desire, even if it's difficult. Dr. Jessica McCleese, an expert of Christian sex therapy says that one way to do this is to acknowledge that our sexual nature is only a small part of who we are; God made us with so many more things!

"When our sexual selves are the focus, we lose who we are as whole people. If we can learn to see ourselves body, soul, and spirit, it becomes easier to save your whole self for marriage, says Dr. McCleese in a published interview online.

DON'T BE AFRAID TO DISCUSS YOUR BOUNDARIES

As much as you are being tempted, you need to discuss your boundaries and standards at least two times that amount. Discussing your boundaries and standards help to re-enforce your beliefs and enable you to stand strong in the Spirit of God against all the temptations that come our way. Timothy 2:22 says, "Flee also youthful lusts: but follow righteousness, faith, charity, peace, with them that call on the Lord out of a pure heart" and setting boundaries and sticking with them would help you do this.

Temptation can have a strong hold in you if you try to battle it on your own strength. However, these strong holds in your life will become weak if you share your struggles openly and honestly with God.

Don't look to other people when you are struggling with temptations in a private setting, look unto the Living God who is able to do abundantly all that we could hope or think (Eph. 3:20). Prayer will also help to remove strongholds in your life. It's okay seek Christians who can give you good advice and can help you pray to get over the temptations you are facing. However, God is the Best Option, as people will always let you down in some way.

ALLOW THE HOLY SPIRIT TO LEAD AND GUIDE YOU

Pray and always ask the Holy Spirit to lead you. Even if you think your to far gone and you know God isn't happy with you, you should continually seek God's repentance, guidance and immerse yourself into the scripture—these things are your best defense against temptation. Galatians 5:16 tells us that we are able to turn away from our sinful nature when we walk in the Spirit. We are able to focus on things that are honest, just, pure, and lovely (Philippians 4:8).

CHAPTER 11: WHAT IF I STUMBLE

IS IT TO LATE BECAUSE OF MY SIN?

Maybe you feel that it's too late. Maybe you feel you've already fallen to deep into sin, and don't think there is still a way out? I remember one song in the 1990's by a Christian rock and rap group DC Talk "What if I Stumble?" and there's one phrase in the lyrics that truly struck me, it was, "I hear you whispering my name 'My love for you will never change.'" This is a great reminder for all of us that even if we fall, even if we are sinning, God's love for us will never change – No Matter What!

"It is because of the Lord's mercies that we are not consumed, because His compassions fail not." Lamentations 3:22

THE FORGIVING FATHER

The parable of the Prodigal Son (Luke 15:11-32) is a story of a man who had two sons. The younger son asked his father to give him the share of his wealth even before his father dies. Of course, we all know that the younger son squandered all his money living the life he wanted, until he ran out of money and began to starve. He was so hungry that even the pods that were given to the pigs looked appetizing to him. This is when he finally came to his senses that he should go home to his father and seek his forgiveness; and so he returned home.

However, even when he was still a long way off from his home, his father already saw him and ran to him to embrace and kiss his son. His father even instructed his servants to dress him with the finest robe, place a ring on his finger and sandals under his feet. He even commanded them to kill the fattened calf and celebrate with a feast.

The older brother on the other hand was angry because his father was celebrating the homecoming of his brother who did nothing but waste his father's money, while he was always faithful in serving his father.

However, his father with this said, "...Son, thou art ever with me, and all that I have is thine. It was meet that we should make merry, and be glad: for this thy brother was dead, and is alive again, and was lost, and is found."

Most people who would come across this parable would focus on the prodigal son's story of repentance, how he admitted his wrongdoings and asked his father's forgiveness.

However, what other miss is the real highlight of this story, which was the prodigal son's forgiving father.

Notice that the father ran to embrace and kiss his son even before the younger son reached their home? If you were in the father's shoes, and your child has asked for his inheritance even before you were dead and then squandered it, would you welcome him back with open arms and throw a feast for him? I bet not. But the forgiving father is a great illustration of how our Father in heaven is.

Our Lord loves us so much that He is more than willing to forgive us and throw a "feast" for us when we repent and ask for his forgiveness. "I, even I, am He that blotteth out thy transgressions for Mine own sake, and will not remember thy sins." Isaiah 43:25

But of course, we don't use the Lord's forgiveness as our license to freely commit sin. For the Lord hates sin.

However, what He wants us to do when we stumble is to confess our sins before Him, ask for restoration, and repent. "If thou return, then will I bring thee again, and thou shalt stand before me…"
Jeremiah 15:19

If you commit sin, you may have to endure the consequences of your actions because our God is a just God. However, if you turn away from sin and ask the Lord for forgiveness and attempt to honor Him with your life, God will surely pour out His blessings upon you. What are the sins that you need to confess to the Lord? Pray and ask for His forgiveness right now.

Chapter 12: Fighting Back

Ways to Fight Back in the Spirit

Now we come to the heart of the matter, fighting back. What does it mean for the Christian to fight back against the onslaught of these demonic forces, specifically regarding 50 shades of gray and all the colors of the Militant LGBT rainbow? Fighting back can take several forms but ultimately starts within the heart of the believer. Many Christians want to focus on the militant LGBT movement and not addressed the lust of the flesh because in doing so they would have to deal with their own issues of sin. For any Christian to start fighting back it's important to have your heart right with God by confessing and repenting onto the Lord Jesus Christ any issues of sin, especially those regarding the lust of the flesh.

The self-reflection can be difficult but it's absolutely necessary to proceed any further in the fight against the demonic forces that use the militant LGBT movement to attempt to destroy what God is created to be holy.

Many people may have bought this book for this specific chapter, to learn how to fight back against those that may be classified as being controlled by demons, potentially even possessed. However, the change you're looking for must start by looking in the mirror and making the change that you want to see. You cannot go into this type of battle, this type of war, with open doors of sinful lust consuming you. These open doors allow demonic forces a spiritual right to claim to certain areas of your life and cause hypocrisy and a reproach because you're not walking in truth, nor the Spirit of God.

GOD'S WAYS VS. THE WORLD'S – WHAT OUR TACTICS SHOULD BE

OPERATE OUT OF LOVE – MATTHEW 5:43-48

Numerous times I've seen video clips of well-meaning Christian believers holding out signs while gathering together and protesting of the militant LGBT community – but I have to ask myself why? This on its surface may seem like a reasonable thing to do yet we must not allow ourselves to use the same tactics that our enemy is using, we have to remember that the world's way and God's way are totally different in all reality.

Take for example those that scream or holler at those that are part of the militant LGBT movement, ask yourself this question, especially if you're one that has done this, is this operating out of the spirit of love for those people? Let me tell you a spiritual secret if you would, intentions committed are felt.

Our spiritual enemy knows this, do you? If you go to a rally or protest and are screaming at those that are ensnared and enslaved by the devil what fruit is that going to bear? Let's flip the scene around a little bit, prior to coming to Christ did anyone scream or holler at you to get you to come to Christ? Is that Jesus's example? Put away the religious façade and ask yourself one question do you hate these people? If your answer is yes to that last question then you need to seek the Lord in prayer and repent because there is none righteous, no not one, there's none who seeks to do good (Romans 3:10-12) – we all have evil in our hearts each and every one of us. And if this is the condition of your heart most assuredly I say unto you, you should not be at any protest or rally as you will only hinder the Spirit of God from reaching these people with the Spirit of love and compassion that Christ has brought to each one of us.

Just remember where you came from prior to accepting the Lord Jesus Christ as your personal Lord and Savior, remember all that he is delivered from, and all that you once were and you most likely will have the love and the compassion necessary to start to share the love of God to those around you including the Militant LGBT community.

Ye have heard that it hath been said, Thou shalt love thy neighbour, and hate thine enemy. But I say unto you, Love your enemies, bless them that curse you, do good to them that hate you, and pray for them which despitefully use you, and persecute you; That ye may be the children of your Father which is in heaven: for He maketh His sun to rise on the evil and on the good, and sendeth rain on the just and on the unjust. For if ye love them which love you, what reward have ye? Do not even the publicans the same? And if ye salute your brethren only, what do ye more than others? Do not even the publicans so? Be ye therefore perfect, even as your Father which is in heaven is perfect.

One of the first and foremost things
that you need to recognize in this war that
you need to operate out of a spirit of love,
for this is Spirit of God. 2 Tim 1:7 says,
"For God hath not given us the spirit of
fear; but of power, and of love, and of a
sound mind." In and of yourself in the
flesh we may not be able to operate with a
spirit of love, however, with God all things
are possible for He gives us His precious
Holy Spirit which enables us to complete
His will – but we must walk in the Spirit.
If we are walking in the spirit of God we
can recognize that those individuals of the
militant LGBT movement are in all
actuality prisoners of their own demise,
slaves to sin, and doomed to an eternal
life of hell without Jesus Christ in their
lives. Let us not be arrogant when
standing strong against the militant LGBT
community for pride surely will come
before fall. But let us with the same loving
grace and mercy that has been shown to
us stand strong in our faith and resolutely
to proclaim boldly the Word of God to a
lost and dying world.

1 Peter 4:8 says, "And above all things have fervent charity (love) among yourselves: for charity (love) shall cover the multitude of sins."

SPEAK IN LOVE

Previously I mentioned those that may holler scream and protest against the militant LGBT community, I won't rehash completely everything I mention before but I want to add here some information that feels vital regarding how to speak in love. For some reason some Christians have the tendency to holler scream at protests and don't recognize their self-defeating actions, in the fact most of their efforts, if not all will not bear any fruit for goes against biblical principles of how to speak and operate in love.

We have to learn to de-escalate situations, this is very important understand, for only when situations become de-escalated that we can have any kind of dialogue that will be productive. For those of you that have led someone to the Lord, in what manner of speech did you lead them?

I can only assume based off of my own experience that it was with the spirit of love and compassion and sincerity that you talked with and prayed with the individual. This is where we need to get to with each other, with the world at large, and of course with the militant LGBT community.

You know love is a verb, it's an action word – it's not something that we just say and then casually go about our day, the word love is a very powerful word that innately requires action from those that speak it or claim it. And we know from 1Corinthians chapter 13 what God's definition of love is – does that mirror our speech and her actions towards those that are enslaved to sin manipulated by demonic forces?

Proverbs 15: 1-2, 14, 18

(v1) A soft answer turneth away wrath: but grievous words stir up anger.

(v2) The tongue of the wise useth knowledge aright: but the mouth of fools poureth out foolishness.

(v14) The heart of him that hath understanding seeketh knowledge: but the mouth of fools feedeth on foolishness.

(v18) A wrathful man stirreth up strife: but he that is slow to anger appeaseth strife..

TRUST IN GOD – HAVE FAITH NOT FEAR

Just about everyone knows the story of David and Goliath even if you're not a Christian but let's examine the story as it pertains to what our tactics should be. First off it's important to note one thing, David was not institutionalized with fear. He did not attend as it were the government-sponsored schools nor was he indoctrinated by his parents to fear the world outside but God alone. In essence David was homeschooled and was taught to have faith in God Almighty, he was taught that there is but one God and He is able, for He is the great I am. Now this is an important thing to remember as it gives insight into how we should raise our own children for the love of God cast out all fear.

Furthermore, God had prepared him in advance for the battle with Goliath with the bear on the lion. God did not just throw David into a situation without preparing him in advance to stand strong against the enemies of God.

Systematically throughout David's life God was building up his faith, his courage, and his physical strength to prepare him for the time to come when he would inevitably stand before the giant.

Psalm 20:7 says, "Some trust in chariots, and some in horses: but we will remember the name of the Lord our God."

Now each of us may have things that we classifies as giants in our life but David stood before an actual giant without fear, without trembling, with godly resolve to defend the honor of God against those that would blaspheme His name.

The militant LGBT movement is a giant demonic force that we as Christians must stand against as David once did against Goliath. Yet the weapons of this warfare are not carnal, but mighty through God to pull down strongholds wherever they may be.

2 Cor. 10:3-5 For though we walk in the flesh, we do not war after the flesh: (For the weapons of our warfare are not carnal, but mighty through God to the pulling down of strong holds;) Casting down imaginations, and every high thing that exalteth itself against the knowledge of God, and bringing into captivity every thought to the obedience of Christ;

Furthermore, the Scriptures declare, "So the Lord said, "If you have faith as a mustard seed, you can say to this mulberry tree, 'Be pulled up by the roots and be planted in the sea,' and it would obey you" (Luke 17:6).

It's a spiritual war at the core, you can spend all day at a protest or rally holding your sign, screaming your head off and basically wasting your time or you can understand the reality of the battle and address it accordingly.

There's a reason that we have the full armor of God – we just have to use it and put it on. We need to understand that this armor is not merely for defense for we have the Sword of the Spirit, which is the Word of God which pierces deep into a man's spirit convicting them of sin. It is said that faith cometh by hearing and hearing the Word of God so it's important as we speak to those enslaved by the devil that we speak to them in love, but what we speak is the word of God.

Zechariah 4:6 says, "Then he answered and spake unto me, saying, This is the word of the Lord unto Zerubbabel, saying, Not by might, nor by power, but by my spirit, saith the Lord of hosts."

A WARNING AGAINST NOT TRUSTING GOD IN THE BATTLE

So how should respond? If we're going to show up we need not show up to protest per se but to pray, to worship, to show forth the love and the glory of our God.

We have to remember the story of Jericho we have to learn from that biblical example. What do we see? We see worship and praise leading the people around the city of Jericho, seven times in fact and then at the conclusion of the seventh lap all those there shouted according to the commandment of the Lord and the walls came tumbling down.

They didn't get preoccupied and focus on their enemy in a physical way, they focused on worshiping and praising the living God and as you know the end result was complete victory.

But the main thing that took place here was that they trusted God and believed that he was able. Again I say the battle is in the spiritual realm and if you truly want to fight back then that means learning more about spiritual warfare and trusting God on a much deeper level than you ever have before your life. A good person to check out as of this writing is Russ Dizdar.

However, those that do not trust God should quite frankly stay home as you will just be in the way and hinder the Spirit of God. The Bible declares that without faith it is impossible to please God, and faith is about trusting Him, and knowing Him to be all that He says he is - capable to do all that we could ever think, see, or ask.

Isaiah 31:1-3 says, "Woe to them that go down to Egypt for help; and stay on horses, and trust in chariots, because they are many; and in horsemen, because they are very strong; but they look not unto the Holy One of Israel, neither seek the Lord!

Yet he also is wise, and will bring evil, and will not call back his words: but will arise against the house of the evildoers, and against the help of them that work iniquity.

Now the Egyptians are men, and not God; and their horses flesh, and not spirit. When the Lord shall stretch out his hand, both he that helpeth shall fall, and he that is holpen shall fall down, and they all shall fail together."

FREEDOM VERSES BONDAGE - JOHN
8:31-34

At what point will Christians stop acting like they are still in bondage, without authority take hold and bind our spiritual enemies? At what point will Christians finally realize who they are in Christ? You are a child of God, a child of the King of Kings and Lord of lords – a Prince or Princess respectively. Do you understand what I'm saying to you right now? You are royalty, you have power and dominion that Christ has given to you you are no longer a slave to sin – act like it. Start "Taking Action for the kingdom of God"

John 8: 31-36 says, "Then Jesus said to those Jews who believed Him, "If you abide in My word, you are My disciples indeed. And you shall know the truth, and the truth shall make you free." They answered Him, "We are Abraham's descendants, and have never been in bondage to anyone. How *can* You say, 'You will be made free'?" Jesus answered them, "Most assuredly, I say to you, whoever commits sin is a slave of sin. And a slave does not abide in the house forever, but a son abides forever. Therefore if the Son makes you free, you shall be free indeed.

DEALING WITH BEING HATED – LEARN FROM JESUS

John 8: 37 – 47 says, "I know that ye are Abraham's seed; but ye seek to kill me, because my word hath no place in you. I speak that which I have seen with my Father: and ye do that which ye have seen with your father. They answered and said unto him, Abraham is our father. Jesus saith unto them, If ye were Abraham's children, ye would do the works of Abraham. But now ye seek to kill me, a man that hath told you the truth, which I have heard of God: this did not Abraham. Ye do the deeds of your father. Then said they to him, We be not born of fornication; we have one Father, even God. Jesus said unto them, If God were your Father, ye would love me: for I proceeded forth and came from God; neither came I of myself, but he sent me. Why do ye not understand my speech? even because ye cannot hear my word. Ye are of your father the devil, and the lusts of your father ye will do.

He was a murderer from the beginning, and abode not in the truth, because there is no truth in him. When he speaketh a lie, he speaketh of his own: for he is a liar, and the father of it. And because I tell you the truth, ye believe me not. Which of you convinceth me of sin? And if I say the truth, why do ye not believe me? He that is of God heareth God's words: ye therefore hear them not, because ye are not of God."

It's clear to see from the Scripture verses that those of the devil operating in sin will not believe the truth and will seek to destroy you if you tell the truth. This is something you should plan for if you plan to attend any gathering in which the opposition will be present. This is why the militant LGBT movement get so enraged at the mere mention of God, the Bible or Jesus Christ. They do not want to remember God or His laws, yet God has written His laws on everyone's heart and there is no escape from the truth that is written therein. This very reason is why most of the Militant LGBT movement are continually frustrated and angry.

Dealing with being hated, despised, or marginalized can be a difficult thing to deal with as we are all human and as such our natural reaction is to lash back out. The psychologically we have to be stronger than that, spiritually we have to be stronger than that, we have to endure hardship as a good soldier of Jesus Christ this is what the word of God commands us to do. It is not glamorous, it is not something to look forward to – although that depends on how you look at it. In the book of acts Peter celebrated that he was counted worthy to suffer tribulation for Christ's sake.

We have to go back to the original doctrine of the apostles, we have to get back to the roots of the core church and understand what that really means. Those not wanting to suffer any persecution tribulation or hard times will be the same ones taking the mark of the beast. What does the Word of God say" And here is the patience of the saints that they did not love their lives on to death", it's by their patients that we possess our souls.

Now does that mean that there is never a time to take up arms physically, of course not – there's a time and place for everything under the sun and a season for everything. However, we have to guard against our love growing cold as I mentioned before, it's the same thing as salt without season. What is a heart without the warmth of the Holy Spirit within it?

For we must burn zealously for the Lord and contend for the faith in every and any possible way we can but we must truly understand that those individuals that we are battling against here on earth are nothing more than puppets of the devil – we have to keep this constant in our mind, we have to understand they're slaves to sin as we once were, bound to eternal damnation without the Lord Jesus Christ in the heart and as such we should have pity on them for without Christ hell is an ever present reality.

Dealing with being hated, once again Jesus is our greatest example on how to deal with this and gives us insight on how to deal with our spiritual enemy as well as our physical enemies. Throughout the New Testament there are numerous examples of Jesus and the disciples being in a situation in which the crowd wanted to seize them and destroy them. Yet what did Jesus do? He came and He said what he had to say and when the crowd became hostile He withdrew, most of the time to the mountains.

So considering the dynamics here with the situation with the Militant LGBT movement, if you going to interact with them (again in a spirit of love) it would be wise to do so and then withdraw because quite frankly your light will drive the demonic forces within them mad and they will ultimately press to destroy you. Unless you are well-versed in spiritual warfare, and the casting out demons I would not recommend interacting to long with those that are clearly oppressed by these forces – again the idea is to de-escalate situations or better yet not have them escalate to begin with.

SHINE THE LIGHT INTO THE DARKNESS

Shining the light into the darkness can be accomplished through various ways I would encourage you to seek the Lord in how you can best shine your light and share your gifts in this dark world. This is one of the greatest things, the Lord gave gifts to men according to His will and good pleasure to serve everyone in the Body of Christ. If you see a need or gap that needs to be filled God may in fact raise you up to shine your light into that dark hole.

DIFFERENCES BETWEEN THE LEFT AND THE RIGHT

There are serious differences between the way that the left and the right go about protesting and effecting change in our society. Time and time again we see the radical left, communist, socialist, and the militant LGBT community using violence and intimidation to affect political change.

Now for those that have a brain and can read this seems to indicate the very definition of terrorism. Yet the politically correct police will never label it as such. The Right believe in the Rule of Law and usually will not go out and riot or create chaos of some kind. Yet the more that they push the right, taking away an infringing on their rights the more likely any group to defend themselves accordingly.

However, Christianity is not a left or right paradigm – it's an up or down paradigm. You're either going to support Biblical principles, and morality in your nation or you're not, but that all starts within your own heart, and dealing with your own sins before God Almighty.

OUR TACTICS

Our tactics should be led by the Holy Spirit and not the desire of any man or woman operating in the flesh. Anything that we do in our own power will not stand against such a vile demonic force. We have to operate with Biblical principles, sound Biblical principles and be led by the Holy Spirit as to the specifics of what to do. Laying out specific tactics here would only nullify our efforts to combat the militant rise of the LGBT movement and the spiritual forces behind it. By enabling the Holy Spirit to lead us and guide us we remain unpredictable to the enemy.

WAYS TO ACTIVELY PROTEST AND FIGHT BACK

One great way to actively protest and fight back against the militant LGBT movement is by pulling your resource together with other believers to leverage greater effects against the enemy. This includes things such as prayer directed at specific targets of the enemy, financial resources to support brothers and sisters out there on the front line, and withdrawing your financial support to those companies that are proclaimed allegiance to the militant LGBT movement.

It's important to pray, fellowship, and plan together with fellow believers and soldiers of Jesus Christ prior to the engagement of any battle. Before every engagement there needs to be a battle plan drawn out with clear objectives to accomplish.

We have to get this notion out of her mind that this is some type of game, this is no game, this is war and believers' need start acting like it if they want to see progress in any way.

The use of alternative media platforms and social media networks are great tool to share the love of God in Jesus Christ. Again one must be strategic about the implementation of using social media networks as many of them will outright ban or censor any material that the Militant LGBT movement may find objectionable. This is why it's critical to utilize platforms in a strategic way while at the same time developing our own platforms and social media networks.

WAYS TO PASSIVELY PROTEST AND FIGHT BACK

A great passive way to fight back against the militant LGBT movement is to have what's called combat force multipliers, which enhance the capability of any one soldier for Christ. Now to those that may have been in the military they understand what this term means yet I am applying it in a spiritual context. What is a spiritual combat force multiplier you might ask – it's quite simple it's brothers and sisters that you have discipled in the faith. The more disciples you create the bleeding and the guiding of the Holy Spirit the more soldiers that are on the battlefield flooding next to you in one accord. This is a great strategy to have because it keeps her eyes fixated on building up the kingdom of God. As a Scripture says, "seek ye the kingdom of God and His righteousness first and all these things will be added onto the"

Another option is to vote if in fact you feel that your vote still counts. I don't personally put too much stock in this but it is an option especially in states that have less corruption. However it deftly is important to hold your so-called elected leaders accountable for their actions in every possible way.

EXAMPLES OF FIGHTING BACK

It seems nowadays the only thing people understand his money, especially losing money. One of the best ways that we as brothers and sisters in the family of God can fight back is by literally making a list of every single company or organization that supports the militant LGBT movement or who penalize in some way those that boldly proclaim their faith. Now individuals should have their own list granted but this list should be put on every Christian website out there as well as passed out in a physical paper form.

For those of you in the alternative media this list should also be on your websites and on a monthly basis at the minimum reference to, to remind Christians to stand strong against the tyranny of oppression by these demonic entities utilizing capitalism for our own demise and enslavement.

Duck Dynasty is a great example of how one network was forced to air this particular show despite opposition from the militant LGBT movement. The simple fact is if Christians pour their dollars into a particular thing that outweighs the militant LGBT movements funding you will have victory – it's simply about the money.

North and South Carolina are also recent examples of ways to fight back in the political world. When men and women of faith and resolve stand up together to proclaim biblical principles on the local level or even the state level much can be accomplished. But we cannot allow our fires to burn out, we have to continually shine the light into the darkness and stay for ever vigilant – this is the price of our freedom, eternal vigilance.

CHAPTER 13: GOD'S BLESSINGS

IT STARTS WITHIN THE HEART OF ONE PERSON

Jeremiah 29:11 says that for I know the thoughts I think towards you thoughts of peace and not of evil to give you a future and a hope. God's desire for us is to live a life of freedom, an abundant life as we serve Him and continually to seek His face on a daily basis. But as you know this blessing can never happen while there's yet sin, like a cancer within you – you have to put on Christ and walk in the spirit of God to be in a position to be blessed. Don't allow yourself because of an unrepentant heart not to receive the blessings of God. Each and every one of us every day needs His protection His provision and of course His love, grace, and mercy. When we are truly seeking the kingdom of God first things will fall into place naturally, without effort and this is the type of life you should seek.

It all starts with the heart, within the heart of the individual lies the keys to unlocking God's blessing for your life. This is not to say that you won't have times of tribulation, times of trouble, or that your life will be smooth sailing. On the contrary anyone that truly is following Christ will be targeted by the spiritual enemy this is something that you should expect and plan for. Yet when you walk with God you're able to bear it, you're able to endure it, you're able to press on and remain forever faithful. Semper Fidelis is what the Marines call it. It's interesting how the Marines have this code of honor God, Family, Country – have you ever heard, read or saw a Christian code of honor that simplifies our belief system like that? I develop something similar a while back for our organization, which is based off of a silver coin, that I purchased some time ago. On the coin was a large tree, it appeared to be an oak tree, and the words Faith, Family, and Freedom were inscribed on it – how fitting is that for code of honor for the Christian believer.

These three simple words can help keep us on track as we battle against the forces of darkness to remain true and faithful to our purpose at hand, to the calling and path God has placed us on, Faith, Family, and Freedom. Powerful words to invoke and to stir the Spirit of God dwelling within you, within your heart so that you can boldly proclaim His Word and not just proclaim it, but walk it out with conviction and compassion and ultimately when you do this you will receive God's blessing.

TO A NATION THAT HONORS HIS WORD

To a nation that horrors God's Word He will continually bless. However, past blessings will never equate to current blessings – it's based on the present circumstances.

We cannot turn her back on God by removing prayer in school, allowing a silent Holocaust to continue caught abortion, and as a nation declare that same-sex marriages are okay and think God's blessing will continue in the United States of America.

However, the Bible declares, "Blessed is the nation whose God is the Lord; and the people whom he hath chosen for his own inheritance" (Psalm 33:12). There is still yet hope in Jesus Christ, "If my people, which are called by my name, shall humble themselves, and pray, and seek my face, and turn from their wicked ways; then will I hear from heaven, and will forgive their sin, and will heal their land" 2 Chronicles 7:14).

A STORY OF GOD'S BLESSINGS

MY NAME IS GABRIELLE, AND THIS IS MY TESTIMONY.

I don't have a tragic story to tell that will bring everybody to tears. In fact, my story might seem ordinary compared to yours, but out of this "plain" story is God's extraordinary blessings pouring out, and I couldn't just sit back and not let everyone know about it.

I grew up in a Christian home. When I was young, I would attend Sunday school every week. There, I learned stories of the "heroes" in the Bible. I learned about Noah and his obedience to God, Moses and the Israelites' exodus from Egypt to the Promised Land, the consequence of Jonah's disobedience to God's command, Jesus' parables and many more. My mom taught me how to pray, and I would always do this before eating, and before going to bed.

However, as I grew older, going to church and praying only became a routine for me. When I was 14 years old, an evangelist from our church visited our home once. For an hour, she explained to me how I needed repent and accept Jesus as my personal Lord and Savior. I couldn't forget that day. That's because even though I have been attending church all my life, it was only then that I understood what salvation really meant. I prayed the sinner's prayer that day and received God's gift of salvation. From then on, I became active in our church. I was involved in several ministries and was able disciple a couple of younger kids attending our church. Then came my senior year in high school.

I met a young man who wished to pursue me and date me. Being surrounded with friends that were already in relationships, I allowed him to court me without the permission of my parents.

My mind was telling me that there's nothing wrong about this since I wasn't jumping into a serious relationship, and I didn't have plans to elope with him in the near future. However, my heart was telling me that I made a wrong decision. Not only because I didn't ask my parents' permission first, but most importantly, because he wasn't a believer.

Being a guy who knows how to swoon me, it didn't take long until we finally called ourselves boyfriend-girlfriend before we graduated high school. We went out on dates, spent most of the time we had with each other before we parted ways because we will be going to different colleges the following school year.

I always prayed to God that I could win him over when I shared the gospel to him. When I had the opportunity, he listened to what I said, but told me that he wasn't ready to become "religious".

Because I was already in love with this guy (or at least I thought I was), I didn't see this as a red flag; I was too blindly in love with him.

However, after several months I noticed that we were starting to become more physical. During the early stages of our relationship, all we did was hold hands, and then he started to hug me, and then kiss me on the cheeks. One time, he tried to kiss me on the lips. I knew in my heart that it was wrong, but I allowed it to happen because I thought I was in love. Then came the time that he was giving me hints that we should "do it". One time, he tried to invite me to his house, only to find out that we were the only ones who will be there.

This was my wake up call. Even though it was hard for me, and it broke my heart, I had to call it quits with him. God made me realized that I was already conforming to the patterns of this world, and that I was playing with fire for too long.

Although I had to endure the pain of letting someone I love go (sleepless nights and endless crying) and although he didn't seem to fully understand my reasons why I was breaking up with him, I felt blessed because God made a way for me to move out of a relationship that would cause me to sin and break my vow to be pure until marriage.

From then on, I focused on my ministry and my studies. Jaci Velasquez' "I Promise" became my favorite song. The lyrics "So I promise to be true to You. To live my life in purity as unto You. Waiting for the day, when I hear You say, here is the one I have created just for you," was written in my heart.

Then my sophomore year in college came. I became very active in one of the organizations in our campus. I was friends with everyone except for this one guy, Matt, whom I didn't seem to notice at all.

Funny thing is, after we were formally introduced to each other, we became inseparable. We became friends, talked and texted almost all the time, and shared stories about all things under the sun. The great thing about him is that he was a believer just like me. In our conversations, we would share about our faith and our experiences in serving God's ministry. And then, the inevitable happened. One day, we both realized that we were starting to like each other, more than just friends.

Coming out of a failed relationship, I knew I had to do it right this time. Matt knew that I believed in courtship so he took the initiative to come to our house and meet my parents. This was his way of asking them and letting them know he wanted to court me. He made it clear to my parents of his intentions and my parents didn't have any problems with this. Knowing that he was a true Christian was enough for them to know that he respects me and is serious about pursuing me.

Of course, Matt and I went out on dates. We enjoyed doing things together like having coffee, walking our dogs in the park, and other activities that couples do. We also tried attending the same church, served the Lord through the music ministry, and would even share the verses we read during our personal quiet time. Even if we considered ourselves as a couple, we both made sure that we won't be in a situation where we will tested to do things that wouldn't please God.

In college having sex when you are in a relationship (or even when you're not) was normal. In fact, everyone we knew had active sex lives. My friends from college who had boyfriends were doing "doing it" like it was no big deal. But, I was blessed that Matt too believed that we should wait until marriage.

No, it wasn't easy for us to remain pure. We were obviously attracted to each other, and there were times that we were tempted to give in, but our prayers and our faith helped us a lot. We would often be teased that we were the only virgin couple in campus, but we didn't care. All we cared about was doing what was pleasing to God's eyes.

It took amazing seven years before Matt proposed for marriage. What impressed me most about him is that he asked my parents' blessing first (without me knowing) before he even asked me to marry him. I would often tease him that he was too confident that I would say "yes" to him. Of course, my parents gave their blessing and of course, I said "yes".

Planning for our wedding wasn't easy because we decided that as a couple, we will be the ones to shoulder the expenses for it.

We knew what we wanted for our dream wedding, but it seemed like we didn't have enough resources to pull it off. We were just starting off with our careers and just had meager savings to pay for a grand wedding. This is when we truly felt God's hand working to make our dream wedding come true. Without even asking, the people close to us would volunteer to pay for some of the costs for our wedding, one even paid for our reception, which was the bulk of our expenses! And I couldn't simply put into words how our wedding turned out to be, the experience was just unforgettable! Almost everyone who attended our wedding was in tears when we exchanged our vows. Our guests said that they truly felt how in love we were and how happy we were to be married; they felt that our marriage was truly blessed by God!

Looking back, I realized that our dream wedding coming to life was only a sample of what God has prepared for us.

Our wedding day was only the surface of one of the best blessing that our Lord has set especially for us—and that was our marriage. Every single day, I would thank God for the chance of waking up beside someone I love. I had the opportunity to serve the Lord with my partner in life. More than having the chance to be physically intimate with my husband, I thank the Lord because He has given me someone whom I can confide with, someone whom I can fight my battles with, and someone whom I can build my dreams with. "I found the one whom my soul loves."

No, Matt and I are not a perfect couple. There are times that we argue even on petty little things, but at the end of the day it is our love for God and love for each other that makes our journey together even more awesome.

I thank the Lord because He gave me a chance to get out of a wrong relationship before it was too late. I thank God because He blessed me with a man He created especially for me. I thank Him because He gave me a man who loved me and respected me. I thank the Lord because he gave us the strength to turn away from temptation and not fall into sin. I thank Him for this because my husband and I can testify that it is possible to remain pure until marriage through the help of God.

My prayer for you is that you remain vigilant and continually seek the Holy Spirit's guidance to help you get through temptation. Yes, it is hard to remain pure until marriage, but we have to claim the Lord's promise in Galatians 6:9 that those who do not faint shall reap a harvest of blessing in God's perfect time.

My story won't hit the box office if it were made into a film, but it's a simple testimony on how God is faithful to those who remain faithful to Him. The Lord has promised immense blessings to those who obey His will, and I've seen it firsthand; He has given my husband and me a great gift of marriage.

CHAPTER 14: CONCLUSION

Its up to each one of us to actively get into the fight, or maybe more importantly realize there is a war going on spiritually and we are all in a battle for our very souls. For the scriptures declare to "Wherefore, my beloved, as ye have always obeyed, not as in my presence only, but now much more in my absence, work out your own salvation with fear and trembling - Philippians 2:12"

This is a real war in the Spiritual realm that continues to bleed over into the physical world. So many men and women of God aren't even in the fight because they refuse to address their sin and run to God for forgiveness, let me tell you now – "As long as there is breath in Your lungs there is Hope in God for Change" – AJF

We must all do what we can, when we can, as God enables us … From personally getting right with God, to effectively leading, guiding and protecting your family, to even effecting you community, society, and ultimately the world. Christians have forgotten what the Militant LGBT community has not – That one person can make a difference in the world and united we become stronger.

Why have Christians forgotten this critical lesson from History – Do we not remember that 12 men (Christ and the 11 Apostles – I don't really count Judas) Changed the World. We as Christian need to walk in that same boldness that they have walked in, that same Spirit of Conviction, Compassion, and Love. There is a time for everything under heaven and as you draw close to Jesus Christ the Holy Spirit will continually lead and guide you. The Question is do you really have Faith –

If you really have Faith you will "Take Action for the Kingdom of God". I challenge the reader to examine if they are in fact in the faith and to walk courageously, yes boldly in the Word of God for His glory sake. If we want to all make America great again then it's going to have to start with a transformation of your heart and the heart of those that claim to follow Christ.

What does the Scriptures say, "If my people, which are called by my name, shall humble themselves, and pray, and seek my face, and turn from their wicked ways; then will I hear from heaven, and will forgive their sin, and will heal their land. 2 Chronicles 7:14" The time is now – "Take Action for the Kingdom of God" and get your heart right before the Lord for tomorrow is never promised.

"Think For Yourself and Learn

Directly From God"

STAY IN CONTACT

OUR CONTACT INFORMATION

Stay in Contact with the American Christian Defense Alliance, Inc. Contactus@acdainc.org Or Email Us Though Our Website At: www.ACDAInc.Org

JOIN OUR MAILING LIST

We also Greatly Appreciate You Signing Up For Our Mailing List and Providing a Good Rating and review for this Book. Your reviews help other people like yourself find this book on Amazon and benefit from its contents.

If You or Your Family have been Blessed by this book please let us know by dropping us a line through our website at http://acdainc.org

Thanks Again for Reading - God Bless!

FIND ALL OUR BOOKS
ON AMAZON

OUR BOOKS ON AMAZON:

Real Men Don't Make Promises:
Understanding Oaths, Pacts, Covenants &
Promises From A Biblical Perspective

Salvation for Your Unsaved Mom: 10
Things to Tell Your Mom Before She Dies

God's Super Minions: Living Faithfully
and Obediently in God

The Perfection of Purity: A Message To
My Daughter

A Vague Notion: How To Overcome
Limiting Beliefs of Fear and Anxiety
Through the Word of God

God's Green Smoothie Book: The Naked Truth

Biblical Bug Out: Don't Bug In - Follow The Calling

Christian Prepping 101: How To Start Prepping

Dirt on Your Tabies: 7 Short Stories of Seisho Ryu Ninjutsu

www.ingramcontent.com/pod-product-compliance
Lightning Source LLC
Chambersburg PA
CBHW031835090426
42741CB00005B/245